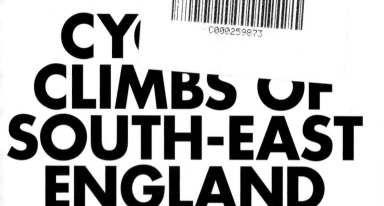

CYCLING CLIMBS OF SOUTH-EAST ENGLAND

A ROAD CYCLIST'S GUIDE

SIMON WARREN

F

FRANCES LINCOLN LIMITED
PUBLISHERS

Frances Lincoln Limited
74–77 White Lion Street
London
N1 9PF
www.franceslincoln.com

Cycling Climbs of South-East England: A Road Cyclist's Guide
Copyright © Frances Lincoln Limited 2015
Text, photographs, design and illustrations copyright © Simon Warren 2015

First Frances Lincoln edition 2015

A catalogue record for this book is available from the British Library.

978-0-7112-3702-5

Printed and bound in China

1 2 3 4 5 6 7 8 9

Thanks to my family and friends for their continued
support, to all the Strava users and Tweeters who
suggested climbs for me to seek out, and to everyone else
who helped bring the book to life.

CONTENTS

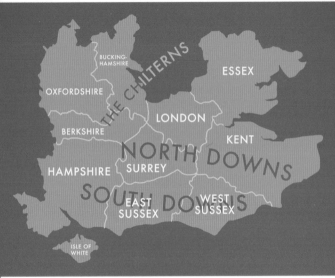

THE SOUTH-EAST

Welcome to *Cycling Climbs of South-East England*, one of eight region-specific guides, packed to the gills with yet more fantastic and challenging British hills.

As you may have already worked out, I've taken the South-East climbs that appeared in my first two British books and amalgamated them into this collection, to quote the marketing department, 'For the very first time, all together in the one place!' But those constitute less than 50 per cent of the volume; there are many more hills, and some real brutes, from areas that I'd criminally overlooked the first time,

such as the South Downs and the far extremities of Kent.

Choosing the remaining climbs was never going to be as easy as compiling the original selection, mind. Like picking the school football team, the star players pick themselves, they are obvious, but with the rest of the pupils lined up how do you decide who fills the remaining places? You have to study each player, judge them on their skill, their athleticism, their willingness, just as you must judge each climb on its length, gradient, and overall riding experience.

As the most populous part of the country, the South-East is naturally home to the busiest roads, but there are many areas of outstanding beauty – where you can experience some peace and quiet – if you just search hard enough to find them that is.

So, where do you go looking for climbs in the South-East? Well, the vast majority of the region's hills can be found peppered along the three vast chalk escarpments that dominate the geography of the region: the Chiltern Hills, the North Downs, and the South Downs. The first of the three, known simply as The Chilterns, runs on a south-west to north-east diagonal from Goring in Oxfordshire right though to Hitchin in Hertfordshire, which belongs to east England so isn't included in this book. Although, having said that, I have taken it upon myself to redraw the nation's geopolitical borders to annex Essex. In an effort to please a few more riders I've assimilated the county into the South-East, removing it from the eastern region, which, let's

face it, will never warrant a volume of its own. So, hard luck Hertfordshire and for that matter Bedfordshire, and welcome to the party Essex.

Going back to The Chilterns, by comparison these are generally, with a couple of exceptions, the easier to ride of the three ranges. Perfect for those still developing their ability to fight the powers of gravity, the climbs are rarely super-steep or especially long.

Moving on to the North Downs, stretching from Farnham, Surrey in the east all the way down to the White Cliffs of Dover in the west, this is by far the longest ridge in the area. The character of this range morphs and adapts as it travels from the congested tangle of the Surrey Hills through the vicious slopes of the Kent Downs to the more gentle climbs approaching the south coast. The area I've spent the most time riding through is the Surrey Hills, and if you're searching for unrelenting climbing set in a labyrinth

of twisting roads, then this is where you want to head. There can be no better introduction to the area than to take part in the annual CTC Cheam and Morden Hilly 50k ride. In its 50 kilometres it packs in over 900m of punishing climbing together with perilous descents to finish at the top of the mighty Box Hill. And if you fancy more of a challenge, then search out the even tougher Tour of the Surrey Hills Audax ride. Its 115-kilometre route manages to climb a whopping 2,300m, taking in four of the climbs in this book.

So finally, the South Downs – having recently been awarded National Park status, this area is a sanctuary from the congestion and overcrowding further north. With climbs set on roads so quiet you can hear a pin drop, surrounded by wide open spaces, fresh air, and stunning, sweeping vistas, they are a joy to ride.

Whilst searching out new climbs, I ended up going over some old ground

to give a few I'd previously documented another look, which in turn led me to question – and in the case of Quell Lane, to alter – my original rating. Initially I'd graded it a 4/10, but I must have been flying that day because on second visit it seemed well shy of the mark so I've moved it up a notch, to a 5/10.

Of all the new hills I found, two really stood out as glaring omissions from my previous books, and they are Firle Beacon and its neighbour Bopeep Bostal. They aren't the easiest climbs to reach as they're stranded on the south coast, but boy is it worth the effort to get there – they are just outstanding. They both lead to nothing but small car parks full of folks unloading dogs from the boots of their vehicles but they optimize what these books are all about: of pushing yourself through the pain barrier to then turn round, basking in your own glory, on top of the world, with a smug smile across your face: you did it.

THE CATFORD AND BEC

So, you think you're pretty handy uphill? You've bagged some KOMs on Strava and shown your mates a clean pair of wheels, but do you have what it takes to pin on a number and line up at a race? Well, if you do, and you live in the South-East, then you must enter the Catford CC and Bec CC hill climbs. Falling on the same Sunday in early October – the Catford in the morning and the Bec in the afternoon – they are an institution not only of local racing, but also of the social cycling calendar. Each year, hundreds of spectators line the narrow hills to scream and shout at the riders, willing them on as they grind against the vicious incline in a struggle to the summit.

The Catford CC hill climb happens to be the longest continually running bike race in history, first held in 1887 when twenty-four hardy souls attacked Westerham Hill on their ancient machines, with the main aim being simply to make the summit. Twelve riders made it that day and from then on, using five different hills before settling on York's Hill in Kent, the event has continued. It was sixty-eight years later that the Bec CC held their first hill climb on White Lane, but the two events are now inseparable – partners in pain.

Now you'll notice I said enter the Catford AND the Bec – this is the important part. No pride can be taken in blasting out a personal best in the afternoon if you haven't first competed in the morning; this is the unwritten rule that all serious competitors must obey. In recent years, the Bec has offered a handsome purse to the winner and this has led some riders to save themselves, to chase the money; but if they win, is it really a victory? Can they look their fellow athletes in the eye knowing they have made only half the effort?

Anyway, many riders swear that the morning's event primes the body for the afternoon; of course others will say it wears you out, but I suppose it depends on how your race goes. If you post a personal best up York's Hill in the morning then that might be you done for the day. On the other hand, if you miss your best, this will fire you up to restore your pride in the afternoon and produce a stellar performance on White Lane.

Now, I have ridden both events every year since 2004 and every time I say 'NEVER again'. But then each October I am drawn to the hills to punish myself once more. I may never go faster, and it's a long time since I have, but where there is hope (and there is definitely hope) there is the will to try. Even with the advancement of age, one year I could just nail it, ride the perfect race. It's true that each time it gets harder for the mind to convince the body to get going, but I won't give up, because if I'm even close to my personal best then that means I'm stalling the ageing process, and I'm still a racing cyclist.

REMEMBER
to check
your bike, check
your body, wear
a helmet, and, above
all, have fun!

LEGEND

UNDERSTANDING THE FACTFILE AND RATINGS

LOCATIONS

You will be able to locate each hill from the small maps provided: simply, **S** marks the start and **F** marks the finish. I would suggest you invest in either Ordnance Survey maps or a GPS system to help plan your routes in more detail. The grid reference in the Factfile locates the summit of each climb, and in brackets is the relevant **OS Landranger** map. The graphic at the start of each chapter will show you where the hills lie in the context of each region.

TIMINGS

Each Factfile includes the approximate time needed to ride each hill. Timed over the distance marked, this is how long it took me to complete each climb at a reasonable, but comfortable pace. Since I rode in all weathers, from blizzards to baking heat, I have adjusted the times slightly to accommodate for the adverse conditions I faced on the day. The times could be used as a target but are really just intended to help you plan your rides.

FACTFILE

WHERE Leave Dorking on the A24 and at the second roundabout past Westhumble exit for Rykers Café. Continue up the B2209 then take the first right to begin.

GRID REF TQ 178 513 (OS187)	
LENGTH 2480m	
HEIGHT GAIN 125m	
APPROX CLIMB TIME 7mins	

RATINGS

The climbs are rated from **1/10** to **10/10** within the context of the book. The rating is an amalgamation of gradient, length, the likely hostility of the riding conditions, and the condition of the surface. All the climbs are tough, therefore **1/10** equals 'hard', and **10/10** equals 'it's all you can do to keep your bike moving'. Some will suit you more than others; the saying 'horses for courses' applies, but all the **10/10** climbs will test any rider.

MAP KEY

Motorway	M1
A Road	A123
B Road	B1234
Minor Road	
Rail line	STATION
Hill route	S START ... F FINISH
Town	TOWN
Scale	2km

LONDON
AND
ESSEX

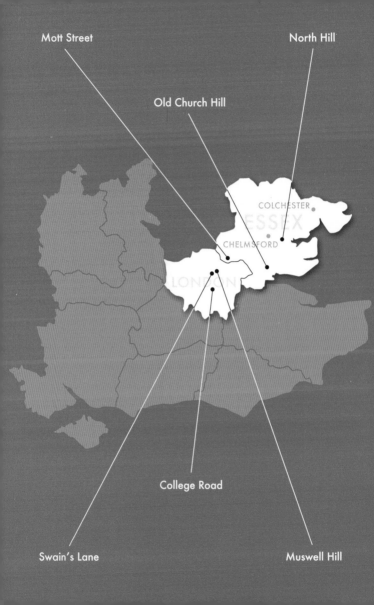

Mott Street

North Hill

Old Church Hill

COLCHESTER

ESSEX

CHELMSFORD

LONDON

College Road

Swain's Lane

Muswell Hill

NORTH HILL

North Hill: the 'Alpe d'Essex' or 'Mont Baddow' – OK, I'm building it up a bit much, but when there's nothing else around, you have to shout about what you've got. Let's make one thing clear, though – this isn't a tough climb. It does, however, draw people from far and wide to ride its slopes and give their best to match the times set by the local talent, and, as I've said many times, any hill ridden hard will hurt you. The climb starts shortly after you cross the River Chelmer at the sign for Little Baddow; narrow but smooth, the first kick up will get you breathing hard, but it's never steep. Through the village the slope hardly wavers from its steady gradient, but the course will get increasingly busy as roads join from the left and the right. At halfway you reach a small junction and the official end to North Hill Road but not the climb; you must continue to push on, now on easier slopes to the top at the junction with the A414 in Danbury.

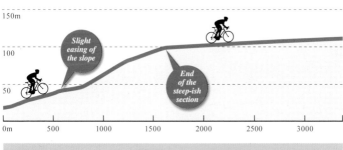

Slight easing of the slope

End of the steep-ish section

FACTFILE

WHERE The base of North Hill lies at the northern edge of Little Baddow which itself lies midway between Danbury on the A414 and the A12.

GRID REF TL 785 057 (**OS**167)

LENGTH 3400m

HEIGHT GAIN 94m

APPROX CLIMB TIME 9mins

OLD CHURCH HILL

LANGDON HILLS, ESSEX

You can see South Hill from miles in all directions. A bold mound rising from the flat plains, it is the Yin to North Hill's Yang, and together they are the hills of Essex. Old Church Hill – the name of the back route up South Hill – is the best way to the top of this peak and what I have documented here. On my first visit I left the T-junction at the base, and, wary of what lay ahead, I ended up spinning a very small gear in anticipation for quite some time waiting for the slope to kick up. In fact it never does kick up, it just gets ever so slightly steeper and steeper until you realize you are running out of sprockets and have to get out of the saddle. Halfway up the hardest stretch, through a clump of houses, there is some respite, and then you are back on it. The narrow surface, continually rough, picks its way up for a hard final push to the top where the South Hill road joins from the right.

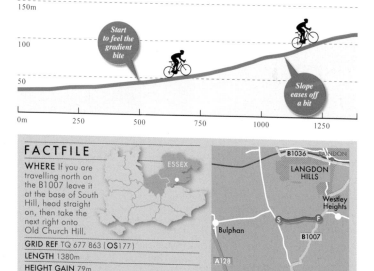

Start to feel the gradient bite

Slope eases off a bit

150m

100

50

0m   250   500   750   1000   1250

FACTFILE

WHERE If you are travelling north on the B1007 leave it at the base of South Hill, head straight on, then take the next right onto Old Church Hill.

GRID REF TQ 677 863 (OS177)

LENGTH 1380m

HEIGHT GAIN 79m

APPROX CLIMB TIME 5mins

ESSEX

B1036 — LONDON

LANGDON HILLS

Westley Heights

Bulphan

S ————— F

B1007

A128

2km

MOTT STREET

Just north of London, in Essex, lies High Beach and the climb of Mott Street. Studying the topography, it's a surprise to find such a tough ascent in this area – there are many shorter hills around, but Mott Street is a proper climb. Begin your ascent at a broken bridleway marker just off the A112. The road bends left, passing the junction to Lippitts Hill, and then rises. A tough opening section flattens where it reaches farm buildings on both sides of the road. A strong whiff of manure is just what you need to propel you up the following lump into the hardest section. The well-surfaced stretch of 12% gradient winds past large gated properties on both sides, levelling slightly half way. The final sector heads into tree cover and the brow comes opposite a bridleway, after which there are just a few hundred metres of false flat before the climb ends at the junction of Church Road.

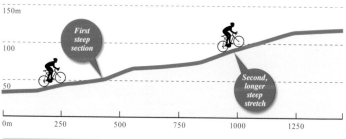

First steep section

Second, longer steep stretch

FACTFILE

WHERE To reach the base head north out of Chingford on the A112. When you reach the village of Sewardstone turn right onto Mott Street.

GRID REF TQ 405 977 (**OS**177)

LENGTH 1460m

HEIGHT GAIN 78m

APPROX CLIMB TIME 6.5mins

RATING
4/10

SWAIN'S LANE

HIGHGATE, LONDON

Of the numerous routes up Highgate Hill, Swain's Lane is the least travelled by
vehicles and one of London's best kept secrets – for cyclists, that is. Start the climb
as the road turns the corner at the base and ride past a right-hand junction. Running
alongside Highgate Cemetery the road is smooth and wide, and what little traffic you
encounter is likely to be travelling past you as the top of the road is one-way. There is a
brief plateau midway past the cemetery gates, and then you are plunged into darkness
as the gradient kicks up. The road is just wide enough for a single car, with a high wall
on the left and thick tree cover overhead. Power up the slope, which touches 20% at its
steepest point. Once past the bespoke house on the left, the gradient eases and a large
radio mast appears. Pass this and finish at the T-junction with South Grove. You've just
conquered Swain's Lane – a proper cycling hill in the capital. Priceless!

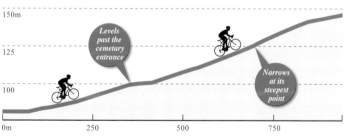

Levels past the cemetery entrance

Narrows at its steepest point

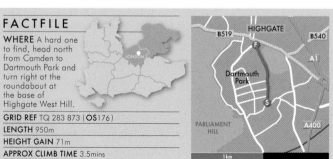

FACTFILE

WHERE A hard one
to find, head north
from Camden to
Dartmouth Park and
turn right at the
roundabout at
the base of
Highgate West Hill.

GRID REF TQ 283 873 (OS176)

LENGTH 950m

HEIGHT GAIN 71m

APPROX CLIMB TIME 3.5mins

MUSWELL HILL

MUSWELL HILL, LONDON

Muswell Hill's a nice place to visit, but you wouldn't want to live here, not if you had to ride to the top of it every day after work! There is little option other than to start the climb from a standstill as you leave the giant junction at the bottom, and right away it settles into its 10% slope. The first 100m are quite narrow then the road widens significantly, and you can ride in the relative sanctuary of the bus lane; running the rest of the way to the top, the lane is a godsend on what can be a very busy road, especially in rush hour. I say the slope is a constant 10%, but in some places it drops to 9% and in others increases to 11%, which makes its modest 650m length seem much, much longer. The road never changes direction – it's just one straight line to the summit, which, together with what you still have to climb, is constantly in view as you toil upwards.

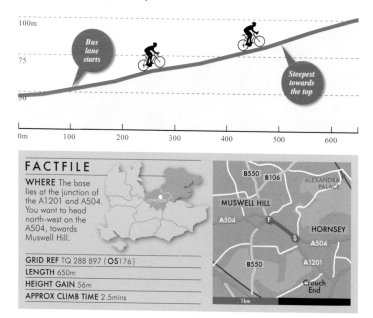

FACTFILE

WHERE The base lies at the junction of the A1201 and A504. You want to head north-west on the A504, towards Muswell Hill.

GRID REF TQ 288 897 (OS176)

LENGTH 650m

HEIGHT GAIN 56m

APPROX CLIMB TIME 2.5mins

COLLEGE ROAD

DULWICH, LONDON

This is my favourite road in south London, and the venue for countless painful hill intervals when I was race training. And why so special? Well, College Road is a toll road, with a booth at the bottom to stop drivers and charge them for the privilege of driving up, which puts many off. This of course makes it much quieter than the other ways up to Crystal Palace and therefore perfect for training. The slope is reasonably steep to begin with, and then you are rewarded with an easing past Sydenham Hill station where you can spin before the gradient bites again. From here, as the road curves right, the gradient increases and you have the added inconvenience of speed bumps to impede your progress. Next the road banks left and becomes Fountain Drive. Here there is a cycle lane protected in places by bollards, and this will take you all the way up to the finish, the hardest part of the climb, to the roundabout at the top.

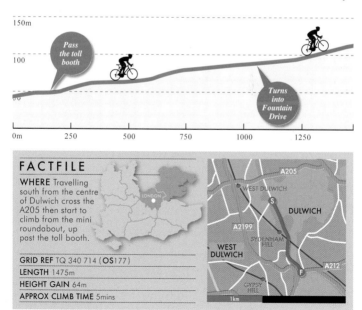

FACTFILE

WHERE Travelling south from the centre of Dulwich cross the A205 then start to climb from the mini roundabout, up past the toll booth.

GRID REF TQ 340 714 (OS177)

LENGTH 1475m

HEIGHT GAIN 64m

APPROX CLIMB TIME 5mins

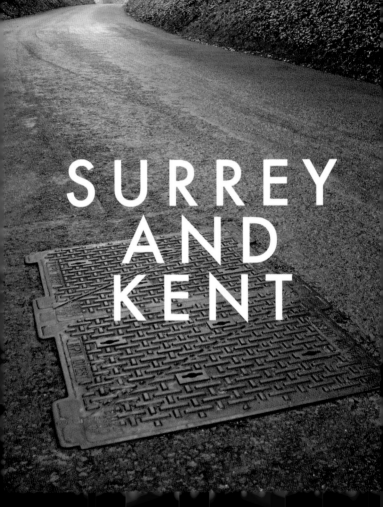

SURREY
AND
KENT

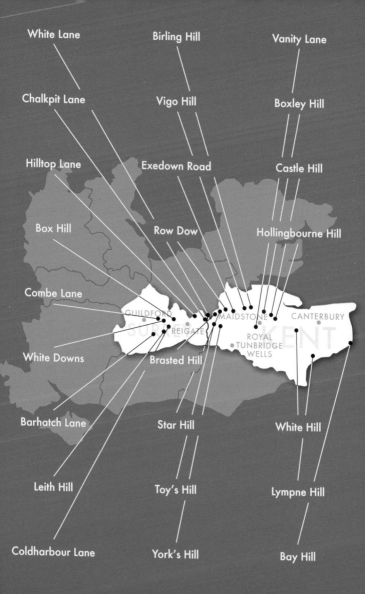

White Lane

Birling Hill

Vanity Lane

Chalkpit Lane

Vigo Hill

Boxley Hill

Hilltop Lane

Exedown Road

Castle Hill

Box Hill

Row Dow

Hollingbourne Hill

Combe Lane

GUILDFORD

MAIDSTONE

CANTERBURY

SURREY

KENT

REIGATE

ROYAL
TUNBRIDGE
WELLS

White Downs

Brasted Hill

Barhatch Lane

Star Hill

White Hill

Leith Hill

Toy's Hill

Lympne Hill

Coldharbour Lane

York's Hill

Bay Hill

BARHATCH LANE

CRANLEIGH, SURREY

Statistically this is the hardest climb in the South-East, and the stats don't lie. If you're not having a good day on the bike, avoid this road – it takes no prisoners. The climb starts at the junction with Amlets Lane, passing first a 21% gradient sign then the Cranleigh Golf and Country Club; the incline is steady. You ride through a tunnel of trees that keeps the road shaded on even the brightest of days, up and up, but it's not yet the 21% advertised at the bottom. When will the steep stuff kick in you ask? Down a slight dip, past various houses and still it's manageable; the trepidation builds – steep, then easing, then steep – it is no killer yet but slowly and surely it's wearing the legs down. Pass a second 21% sign and here it is, the remorselessly tough top section. This has to be steeper than 21% – it must be 25% – you have to make it to the brow at the top and just hope you have a gear low enough.

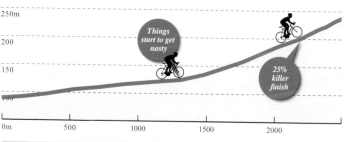

250m

200

150

0m   500   1000   1500   2000

Things start to get nasty

25% killer finish

FACTFILE

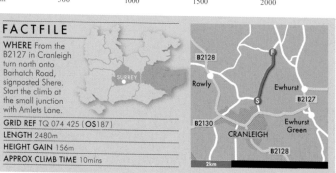

WHERE From the B2127 in Cranleigh turn north onto Barhatch Road, signposted Shere. Start the climb at the small junction with Amlets Lane.

GRID REF TQ 074 425 (OS187)

LENGTH 2480m

HEIGHT GAIN 156m

APPROX CLIMB TIME 10mins

B2128
Rowly
SURREY
Ewhurst
B2127
B2130
Ewhurst Green
CRANLEIGH
B2128
2km

COMBE LANE

SHERE, SURREY

This is a kinder ride up the North Downs than the infamous White Downs to the east, but nonetheless one with a real sting in its tail. Leave the village of Shere from its western exit, cross the A25 and the climb starts immediately from the main road. It doesn't hit you right away. You have plenty of time to get used to the incline, up to the first serious bends, left then right, now you know you're climbing. Next you have a long straight; up ahead you see the road bend right and climbing is noticeably tougher. You'll now need to click up a couple of sprockets to preserve a good cadence and continue to bend right pushing on up to the finale. This is where you will need to get out of the saddle and give it everything round the last bend into the final short stretch. It's a super-tough left-hander into a super-tough ramp. Follow the road up to the sharp right-hand corner, and then finish at the brow where the slope ebbs away.

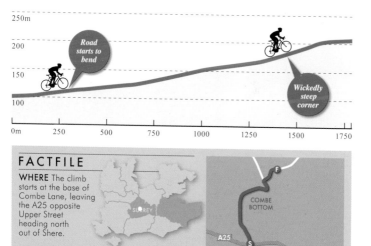

Road starts to bend

Wickedly steep corner

FACTFILE

WHERE The climb starts at the base of Combe Lane, leaving the A25 opposite Upper Street heading north out of Shere.

GRID REF TQ 074 494 (OS187)

LENGTH 1785m

HEIGHT GAIN 108m

APPROX CLIMB TIME 8mins

WHITE DOWNS

DORKING, SURREY

Starting from the A25 and rising to cross the Pilgrims Way along the North Downs, White Downs is an obligatory inclusion on local cyclosportive routes. The road ascends immediately, but what you are presented with at first are best described as two false starts as the road rises, levels out, rises again, and then descends. Your heart rate will be up and legs primed, but the climb proper doesn't begin until you cross the railway bridge at roughly halfway. Now it really gets tough as the gradient increases slightly, then – bang! – you're faced with two hairpins, first left, then right, and both 20% at the apex to stop you in your tracks. Next comes a long, gruelling slog up the steep but smooth climb, where the sides of the road are littered with rocks of chalk. As you approach what appears to be the summit you round a final left turn to face another excruciating 50m before you have conquered this beast of the South-East.

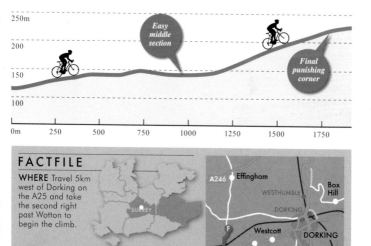

FACTFILE

WHERE Travel 5km west of Dorking on the A25 and take the second right past Wotton to begin the climb.

GRID REF TQ 114 490 (OS187)

LENGTH 1900m

HEIGHT GAIN 121m

APPROX CLIMB TIME 8mins

LEITH HILL

DORKING, SURREY

The proud owner of the highest point in the South-East, Leith Hill is one of the longer climbs on the North Downs and a road that is raced many times each year, making and breaking riders' reputations in the process. Leaving the B2126 you have a couple of hundred metres in which to choose your gear and prepare for the ascent. Following a footpath on the right, you climb steeply at first and then you are allowed a slight respite before the road's abrasive surface starts eating into your reserves once again. It's steep here and framed with high brick walls that follow the still-steepening rise, which turns first right, then left, where you climb towards an intersection of three roads that form a triangle. Bearing left here you have a chance to ease up slightly. But it's not for long, as once again the road climbs and you follow it round to the right, drained from the seemingly endless grind, to the car park on your right.

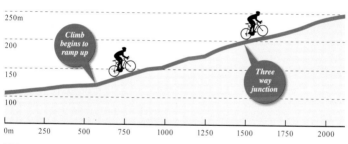

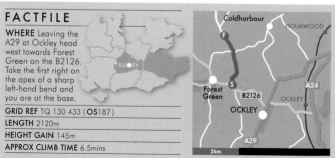

FACTFILE

WHERE Leaving the A29 at Ockley head west towards Forest Green on the B2126. Take the first right on the apex of a sharp left-hand bend and you are at the base.

GRID REF TQ 130 433 (OS187)

LENGTH 2120m

HEIGHT GAIN 145m

APPROX CLIMB TIME 6.5mins

COLDHARBOUR LANE

DORKING, SURREY

Even on the brightest summer's day it's dark on Coldharbour Lane, which lies at the bottom of a canyon-like trench lined with 5m-high dirt walls under a tall canopy of thick forest. From Dorking, leave the A25 on to Falkland Road and then over a small bump before dropping to level past farm buildings: this is where the climb truly begins. Easing your way up the incline, it's hard, getting harder under the trees before backing off a little, then hard again to the junction on the right. The claustrophobic banks are now growing around you and the road kinks slightly left to continue its gloomy journey along the debris-covered surface. The name of the road changes briefly past the junction, to Boar Hill, and this feels like the toughest stretch of climbing. As soon as the gradient recedes, you return to Coldharbour Lane to continue the lumpy journey to the summit shortly before you roll down into Coldharbour itself.

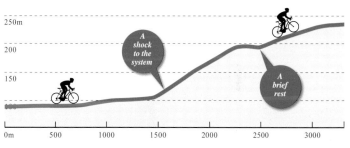

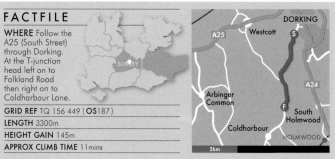

FACTFILE

WHERE Follow the A25 (South Street) through Dorking. At the T-junction head left on to Falkland Road then right on to Coldharbour Lane.

GRID REF TQ 156 449 (OS187)

LENGTH 3300m

HEIGHT GAIN 145m

APPROX CLIMB TIME 11mins

BOX HILL

DORKING, SURREY

A lot has happened to the humble Box Hill since I first wrote about it. It is now known the world over thanks to its appearance as the showpiece of the 2012 Olympics road race. Although fame quickly fades, what will last longer is the fresh, silky surface it received for the games, and today it is probably the smoothest climb in all of Surrey. The aptly named Zig Zag Road leaves the B2209 and begins its ascent beneath a thick canopy of trees. The gradient is steady but significant then levels briefly at the first hairpin, which has the effect of slingshotting you around the bend. To maintain speed, hug the left-hand gutter and hold your line to the second hairpin. Steep through the bend, you exit the tree cover to begin the longest stretch, which can be especially tough in a headwind. Looking right you'll see the valley below before you enter the trees again for the final right-hand bend and push for the café at the top.

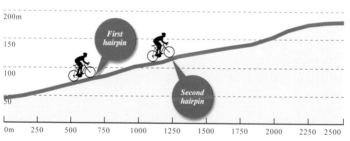

FACTFILE

WHERE Leave Dorking on the A24 and at the second roundabout past Westhumble exit for Rykers Café. Continue up the B2209 then take the first right to begin.

GRID REF TQ 178 513 (OS187)

LENGTH 2480m

HEIGHT GAIN 125m

APPROX CLIMB TIME 7mins

HILLTOP LANE

MERSTHAM, SURREY

Once a year I like to ride from my east London home to Brighton and back, and on the return leg it's always this hill that finishes me off. It doesn't help that I hit it with 150 kilometres under the belt but even with fresh legs it hurts, and anyway the ride would not be complete without it. The punishment comes in three waves. First there is a small rise away from the junction at the bottom, before it levels across the giant, sprawling junction of the M23 and M25. Next is the hardest stretch, straight and very steep, and then after a couple of hundred metres you get a breather before the road bends left and the serious climbing starts again. Getting harder all the time, up ahead the killer finale comes into view, and this is why this road is special. Bending right and disappearing out of sight is one hell of a steep corner – I've seen grown men weep trying to force their smallest gear over to make it round and to the top, just a few metres further on.

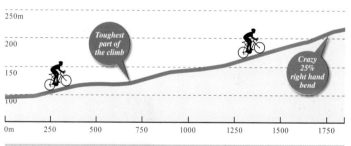

Toughest part of the climb

Crazy 25% right hand bend

FACTFILE

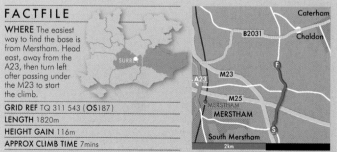

WHERE The easiest way to find the base is from Merstham. Head east, away from the A23, then turn left after passing under the M23 to start the climb.

GRID REF TQ 311 543 (OS187)

LENGTH 1820m

HEIGHT GAIN 116m

APPROX CLIMB TIME 7mins

CHALKPIT LANE

LIMPSFIELD, SURREY

This is my favourite road in the South-East. Why? I don't know, as I always suffer like a dog on it. The climb is gentle at first as you leave Limpsfield, but above you the vertical chalkface that dominates the skyline awaits. Make the most of the early slopes – they don't last. Passing beneath the monumental square bridge under the M25, the gradient starts to bite, still not terrible but enough to quicken the breathing and lower the gears. Bending left past the first entrance to the chalkpit, you now know you're on a proper hill. Ahead, the wicked right-hand hairpin comes into view and from there begins the toughest stretch. Grind round the corner and begin an achingly uniform 20% slog on the perfectly surfaced road. Dead straight, you are offered no respite for over 200m before it gradually bends left and thankfully finishes at the T-junction. OUCH.

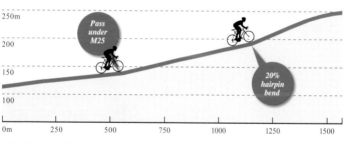

Pass under M25

20% hairpin bend

FACTFILE

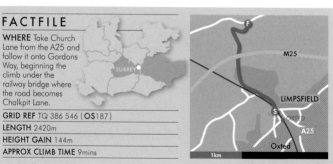

WHERE Take Church Lane from the A25 and follow it onto Gordons Way, beginning the climb under the railway bridge where the road becomes Chalkpit Lane.

GRID REF TQ 386 546 (OS187)

LENGTH 2420m

HEIGHT GAIN 144m

APPROX CLIMB TIME 9mins

WHITE LANE

LIMPSFIELD, SURREY

Known also as Titsey Hill owing to the fact it runs parallel to the B269 of that name, the narrow White Lane is the cyclist's preferred route up this ridge. The climb starts as soon as you leave the main road, rising steeply at first before shallowing slightly, then rearing up with a vengeance near the end. It's a short climb, but a feared one nonetheless as it's the venue for the famous Bec Cycling Club's annual hill climb. Its surface is rough, pitted, and stained white at the edges by the chalk that washes from the surrounding North Downs. Riders are faced with a real struggle to build early momentum as the first two-thirds of the climb are very abrasive and hard going on the tyres. Following a speed-bump-like imperfection caused by poor road maintenance at roughly half distance, the surface improves, but here the gradient also increases as it climbs viciously through a tunnel of tree cover to the crest.

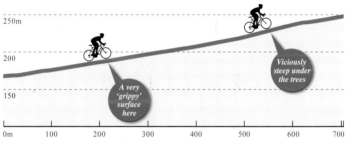

A very 'grippy' surface here

Viciously steep under the trees

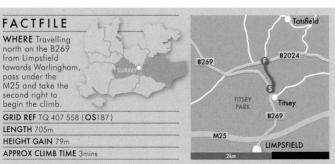

FACTFILE

WHERE Travelling north on the B269 from Limpsfield towards Warlingham, pass under the M25 and take the second right to begin the climb.

GRID REF TQ 407 558 (**OS**187)

LENGTH 705m

HEIGHT GAIN 79m

APPROX CLIMB TIME 3mins

RATING
5/10

BRASTED HILL

BRASTED, KENT

Brasted Hill was the venue for the very first UK national hill climb championship back in 1944 won by Frank Worthen, and also used twenty-one times as the venue for the famous Catford CC Hill Climb, although on a shorter distance than I have documented here. The climb is very gentle to begin with, rising out of the village under the M25, and it's not until you cross the Pilgrims Way that the pain starts. Standing in front of you it appears a fearsome obstacle, dead straight, punishingly steep and you're forced to shift a whole handful of sprockets before you can continue. With no variation in severity or direction, it is a huge relief when the corners arrive, just to get you away from the gruelling monotony of that 15% straight. The change in direction takes the edge off the effort, first right then left, leading you to the remainder of the ascent, which, like the start, is very gentle up to the right-hand bend that marks the summit.

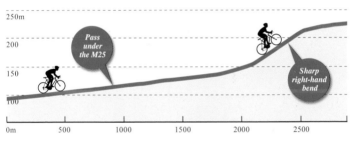

250m

200

150

100

Pass under the M25

Sharp right-hand bend

0m   500   1000   1500   2000   2500

FACTFILE

WHERE The climb rises out of Brasted. If you enter the village from the East take the first right onto Rectory Lane then head on up.

GRID REF TQ 462 576 (**OS**188)

LENGTH 2890m

HEIGHT GAIN 140m

APPROX CLIMB TIME 8mins

Knockholt

F

PILGRIMS WAY

M25

A25

Westerham

B2211

Sundridge

S

BRASTED

2km

KENT

STAR HILL

KNOCKHOLT POUND, KENT

Good times, bad times – I've had them all on this climb, which forms the finale to the annual Sydenham Wheelers Reliability Trial. At the end of 100 kilometres of hard riding and sharing the pace with your clubmates, you arrive at the base where all loyalties and bonds are forgotten: it's now everyone for themselves. Hostilities begin as you leave the roundabout on the A224 where the road climbs gently up to the left-hand bend, through this and it gets steeper and steeper. Click down the gears, try to stay with your mates, and no matter how much you are suffering endeavour to show no pain. By the time it banks right you've reached the halfway point so now it's time to turn the screw, to attack the summit. It is here in this last stretch, past the houses, where the damage is done, where you can strike that psychological blow by riding away solo or, on the other hand, get dropped like a stone to arrive crestfallen.

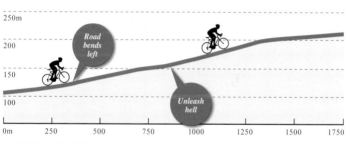

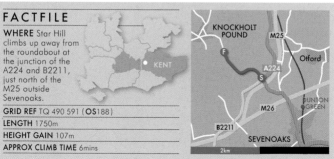

FACTFILE

WHERE Star Hill climbs up away from the roundabout at the junction of the A224 and B2211, just north of the M25 outside Sevenoaks.

GRID REF TQ 490 591 (OS188)

LENGTH 1750m

HEIGHT GAIN 107m

APPROX CLIMB TIME 6mins

TOY'S HILL

EDENBRIDGE, KENT

A long, arduous ascent by South-East standards, so don't be fooled by its playful name – this climb is as serious as it gets along the North Downs ridge. Leaving the B2042 in the valley, north-east of Edenbridge, Toy's Hill bears slightly left, climbing gently at first, with the gradient gradually increasing in definite segments until you hit the final 18% push to the summit. Keep some strength in reserve until you see the village of Toy's Hill, where the effort really kicks in. The death blow comes in the shape of 300m of dead straight, silky smooth tarmac that saps every last ounce of strength from the legs. As you pass the sloping driveways of the houses on your right, you'll be begging for the end, but it doesn't come easy: there's still a good 200m following the steepest section before you can finally relax at the crest adjacent to the Toy's Hill car park.

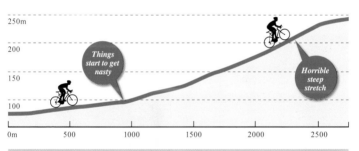

Things start to get nasty

Horrible steep stretch

FACTFILE

WHERE 3km east of Edenbridge pass through Four Elms and leave on the B2042 heading north-east. Take the first left to begin the climb.

GRID REF TQ 470 518 (OS188)

LENGTH 2650m

HEIGHT GAIN 176m

APPROX CLIMB TIME 9mins

YORK'S HILL

SEVENOAKS, KENT

York's Hill is famous for being the course of the oldest bike race in the world: the annual Catford CC Hill Climb. Each year in October, the final metres of this hill are lined five deep with screaming supporters willing competitors on as they wrench their bikes up the 20% gradient to the finish line. For a couple of hours it's as if the Tour de France itself has been transposed to deepest Kent where those competing get to experience what it feels like to race through a throng of rampant fans. But York's Hill is far steeper than the Alps. This testing, twisting climb with its deteriorating topping will tear your legs off. The lower slopes, strewn with the debris that washes on to the road from the high, tree-lined banks either side, force you to search for the cleanest line to get enough traction as the gradient increases. The road switches left to right, left and right again, and relief comes only at the end as you reach Goathurst Common.

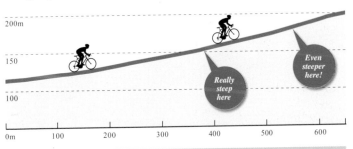

FACTFILE

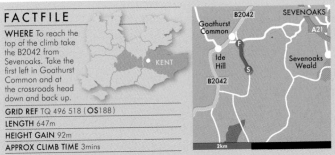

WHERE To reach the top of the climb take the B2042 from Sevenoaks. Take the first left in Goathurst Common and at the crossroads head down and back up.

GRID REF TQ 496 518 (OS188)

LENGTH 647m

HEIGHT GAIN 92m

APPROX CLIMB TIME 3mins

ROW DOW

This is a hard climb but not as hard as I was expecting given its fearsome reputation. I arrived ready for some painful 20%, but alas, all it had to offer was 14% slopes. On the plus side they are long 14% slopes so don't for a moment think it will be easy. Leaving the Pilgrims Way, just east of Otford, it rises abruptly, so engage a small gear on your approach to save you stalling as soon as you hit the base. Up past the manicured and well-equipped grounds of the exclusive-looking Woodlands Manor School, the slope backs off briefly, offering a last chance to relax before you begin the intimidating path ahead. Rising up through the trees, this is where it gets hard – there are no bends or corners to ease the suffering, it's just straight up and steep. As the high banks subside and chinks of daylight appear through the canopy overhead you are approaching the summit, which arrives at the junction with Birchin Cross Road.

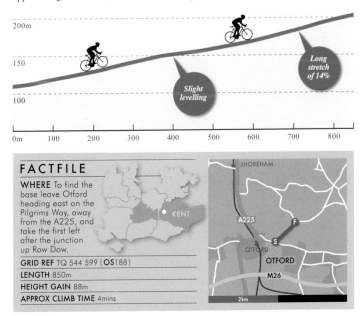

Slight levelling

Long stretch of 14%

FACTFILE

WHERE To find the base leave Otford heading east on the Pilgrims Way, away from the A225, and take the first left after the junction up Row Dow.

GRID REF TQ 544 599 (**OS**188)	
LENGTH 850m	
HEIGHT GAIN 88m	
APPROX CLIMB TIME 4mins	

RATING
5/10

EXEDOWN ROAD

WROTHAM, KENT

Sandwiched between the M26 and the M20 lies Exedown Hill, home of, in my opinion, the best corner in Kent. The road rises all the way from Igtham up Fen Pond Road, passing under the M26, but the 'climb' doesn't really start until you reach the junction with Kemsing Road. Dead ahead you see a large radio mast sitting on top of the ridge, and over to your right the chalk cliffs peaking though the grassy banks. The road climbs, leans right, and then you reach 'the' corner where it banks sharp left, almost 180 degrees like a proper mountain hairpin. You are duly delivered on to an arduous stretch of climbing: an unrelenting 10% slope that takes you all the way to where the road kinks right, eases, then sweeping back left eases again. If I was planning a route round here, then this hill would be on it every time; what a climb, and the views of the Kent countryside from the top are a fantastic reward for your effort.

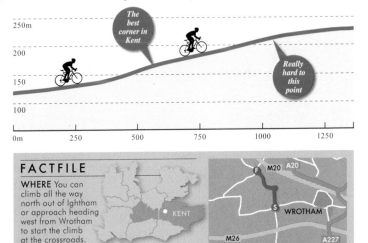

FACTFILE

WHERE You can climb all the way north out of Ightham or approach heading west from Wrotham to start the climb at the crossroads.

GRID REF TQ 588 602 (**OS**188)

LENGTH 1510m

HEIGHT GAIN 106m

APPROX CLIMB TIME 5mins

VIGO HILL

RATING
7/10

VIGO HILL

TROTTISCLIFFE, KENT

I'm calling the start as the small triangular green in the quaint village of Trottiscliffe. Note the word 'cliff' hidden in there – I do hope you've packed your climbing gear. Rolling up past picturesque oast houses, the start is busy, with differing gradients, speed bumps, and many iron grilles. Up to the steep left-hand bend, the surface is in places immaculate, which is a miracle for Kent as most of its roads resemble little more than farm tracks. It's tough round the bend and only gets tougher past a battered and faded 1:6 gradient sign. Up ahead the climb ramps skywards, with dark tarmac set on an arching camber dotted with huge iron plates. Aim for the bridge on the horizon because that's the top. Well, it's not, I just said that to make it sound easier. You've got to drag yourself under, keep the gear turning, and, after an age on the constant 1:6 slope, it finally ebbs away to end at the junction on the outskirts of Vigo.

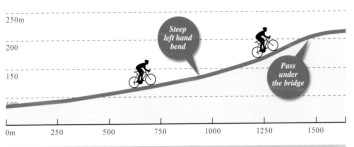

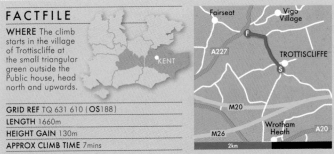

FACTFILE

WHERE The climb starts in the village of Trottiscliffe at the small triangular green outside the Public house, head north and upwards.

GRID REF TQ 631 610 (OS188)

LENGTH 1660m

HEIGHT GAIN 130m

APPROX CLIMB TIME 7mins

BIRLING HILL

BIRLING, KENT

This climb goes on and on: it is a hard, claustrophobic struggle up a dirty and relentlessly steep slope to the summit. It's not all tough, mind, although at the base, where Stangate Road leaves Snodland Road, there is a sharp kick before it settles down on the long approach to the ridge ahead. For close to a kilometre the tension builds. Shake the legs, have a drink, a bite to eat maybe, because once you pass under the cover of trees you've a proper fight on your hands. Up and up, set on a solid 10% slope you pick your way between the high muddy banks, trees perched, clinging to the tops, their exposed roots falling to the edge of the tarmac. You ride trapped, allowed only fleeting glimpses of Kent's finest scenery through the bar-like branches that imprison you on the punishing slope. Your struggle to the top is now also your struggle for daylight which you find only as you reach the house that marks the summit.

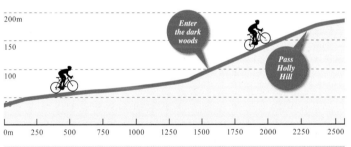

FACTFILE

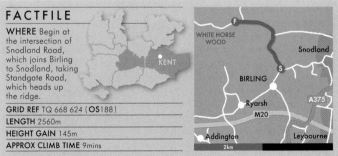

WHERE Begin at the intersection of Snodland Road, which joins Birling to Snodland, taking Stangate Road, which heads up the ridge.

GRID REF TQ 668 624 (OS188)

LENGTH 2560m

HEIGHT GAIN 145m

APPROX CLIMB TIME 9mins

VANITY LANE

LINTON, KENT

Along this ridge you have, from west to east, four killer hills very close to each other: Hunton Hill, Westerhill Road, Vanity Lane, and Linton Hill. I rode them all, digested my findings and picked a favourite – Vanity Lane – and not just because it had the best name. To find the start you'll either have to descend, or begin to climb the very busy Linton Hill to the turn off on to Wheeler's Lane, which leads to the base. You begin the climb between towering hedgerows and the slope is easy at first, up to and past a few houses, then passing the last one the road disappears skyward under the cover of trees. Horribly rough, covered in debris, it is a fearsome gradient, rising dead straight, on and on and passing beneath a somewhat bizarre footbridge that links the high banks either side of you. Under this and there's still a lot more hard climbing to come, almost all the way to the finish, which lies just shy of the junction at the top.

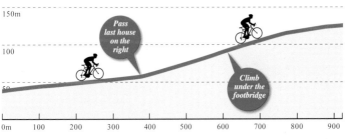

FACTFILE

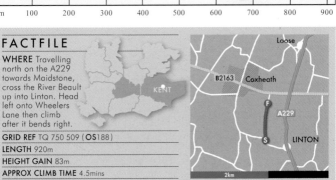

WHERE Travelling north on the A229 towards Maidstone, cross the River Beault up into Linton. Head left onto Wheelers Lane then climb after it bends right.

GRID REF TQ 750 509 (**OS**188)

LENGTH 920m

HEIGHT GAIN 83m

APPROX CLIMB TIME 4.5mins

RATING
7/10

BOXLEY HILL

BOXLEY, KENT

Sweeping down out of Maidstone, the ridge ahead appears a formidable obstacle with its sheer chalk walls grinning through the thick tree cover. Begin the climb as the wide road snakes through the valley away from the M20, and then starts to rise up towards Boxley. Banking right, you enter the village and there's a momentary plateau through some traffic calming; the road then narrows, squeezes, so take care here. Out the other side and the slope increases to the point where the climb assimilates a stretch of the Pilgrims Way. Now almost level, looking left you can cast your eyes over Maidstone in the valley before banking hard right, and then the proper climbing begins. Winding gradually left and right you grind up through the 17% strength-sapping curves. Each bend delivers tougher climbing up to two giant chalk buttresses that lie either side of the road, like gates marking the approach to the summit.

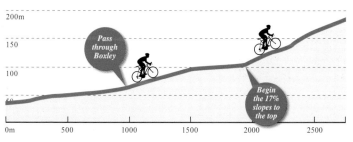

FACTFILE

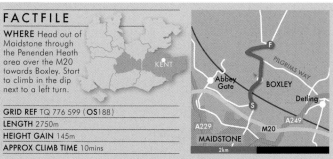

WHERE Head out of Maidstone through the Penenden Heath area over the M20 towards Boxley. Start to climb in the dip next to a left turn.

GRID REF TQ 776 599 (OS188)	
LENGTH 2750m	
HEIGHT GAIN 145m	
APPROX CLIMB TIME 10mins	

RATING
5/10

CASTLE HILL

THURNHAM, KENT

Riding along the Pilgrims Way, chances are you'll ride straight past this road. It's a road to nowhere, but well worth the diversion. In fact, the ludicrously steep left-hand bend that lies on its upper slopes is alone more than worth the journey. Begin the climb as Thurnham Lane passes under the M20 heading north-east, and the road very gradually begins to rise. It's not until you approach Thurnham that the slope starts to bite, though, and not until you cross the Pilgrims Way that it starts to hurt. Here is what you came for as the narrow dead end picks its way under the dark cover of trees. Then up ahead you see light at the end of the tunnel of foliage and catch sight of that fantastic corner that you've come to ride. Heave yourself left and continue up on the draining gradient, which continues until the road breaks right, and with the hard work behind you, you pass the ruins of the castle and come to a halt as the tarmac ends.

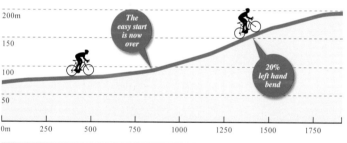

The easy start is now over

20% left hand bend

FACTFILE

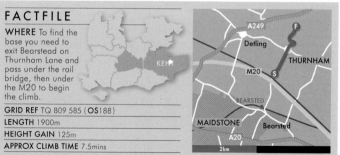

WHERE To find the base you need to exit Bearstead on Thurnham Lane and pass under the rail bridge, then under the M20 to begin the climb.

GRID REF TQ 809 585 (OS188)

LENGTH 1900m

HEIGHT GAIN 125m

APPROX CLIMB TIME 7.5mins

HOLLINGBOURNE HILL

HOLLINGBOURNE, KENT

Hollingbourne Hill or the QHC/11 is the venue for the annual Wigmore CC Hill Climb, which, starting from the junction with the Pilgrims Way, is not the distance I have measured here but slightly shorter. I've called the base the levelling in front of the All Saints Church; following this, you bend right into the village and begin to rise up past The Dirty Habit inn. Crossing the Pilgrims Way, the wide, smooth road continues upwards but the gradient is tame, for now. Your main obstacle on the lower slopes is the heavily set ironworks that force you out of the gutter, so take care when manoeuvring. When the road kinks first left then right, there is a definite change under your tyres; now it's hard, and it gets harder, ramping up incrementally towards the visible brow. Go too deep too early and these later 12% slopes will eat you up, so measure your effort to finish just past the entrance to Hollingbourne House.

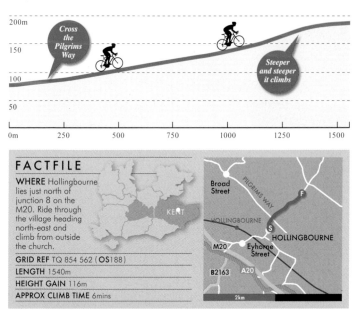

FACTFILE

WHERE Hollingbourne lies just north of junction 8 on the M20. Ride through the village heading north-east and climb from outside the church.

GRID REF TQ 854 562 (OS188)

LENGTH 1540m

HEIGHT GAIN 116m

APPROX CLIMB TIME 6mins

RATING
4/10

WHITE HILL

CHALLOCK, KENT

I rode this climb in a road race once. We waited the whole 100 kilometres for this hill, for our faux mountaintop showdown, and it didn't disappoint, although, unfortunately, I did. Heading away from the A28, and up ahead you see the ridge of flowing, interlocking hills: if you have the gears and have the legs you should be able to stay seated until you cross them. Gentle at first, then the gradient picks up past a farm and continues tough between the high, wooded banks. Riding further, the slope gradually ebbs away up to the first of two car parks where it seems to disappear, but you're still climbing, and this isn't the top. Engage the big ring here and pick up speed through an avenue of trees as the road meanders left and right to the finale. This comes in the form of a sharp little ramp, a real sting in the tail, but stay in the big ring, crush it with your power, then you'll cross the brow at the large King's Wood car park.

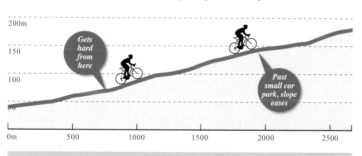

Gets hard from here

Past small car park, slope eases

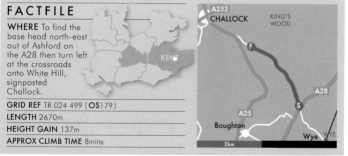

FACTFILE

WHERE To find the base head north-east out of Ashford on the A28 then turn left at the crossroads onto White Hill, signposted Challock.

GRID REF TR 024 499 (OS179)

LENGTH 2670m

HEIGHT GAIN 137m

APPROX CLIMB TIME 8mins

RATING
4/10

LYMPNE HILL

WEST HYTHE, KENT

Lympne Hill begins in the tiny village of West Hythe, which lies just inland from what was once dubbed the 'smugglers coast', to the west of Folkestone. Crossing the Royal Military Canal, which was built to stop Napoleon, and up ahead the ridge looms high above you, a mighty wall you must scale. The first slopes are the hardest as the road ramps up, but since the legs will be fresh they will cope with the gradient. Just at the point when they want to scream, though, thankfully the slope backs off. You'll not notice it at first but soon you'll feel yourself pedalling freely, so click down a sprocket. Through the slightly easier middle section, and avoiding the large ironworks, you pass a footpath sign and it becomes a struggle again. Up ahead you'll see a road sign peak out over the horizon: as it marks the top, this is your carrot – so chase it. Once there, you'll see the 14% gradient sign – 14%! It felt much tougher than that in places.

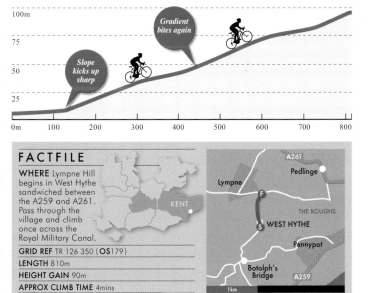

FACTFILE

WHERE Lympne Hill begins in West Hythe sandwiched between the A259 and A261. Pass through the village and climb once across the Royal Military Canal.

GRID REF TR 126 350 (OS179)

LENGTH 810m

HEIGHT GAIN 90m

APPROX CLIMB TIME 4mins

BAY HILL

ST. MARGARET'S BAY, KENT

Lying just 34 kilometres from the coast of France, St Margaret's Bay marks the narrowest point on the Straits of Dover. And here, in this tiny settlement, at the very extremities of South-East England lies a wicked, twisting little hill. When you arrive in St Margaret's at Cliffe, pass through the village on Sea Street and down Bay Hill to the Shore. Take in the view, maybe even go for a swim, and then turn around to climb back up. Right away it's hard to the first hairpin, then eases as it rounds to the right and up past the grand houses that line the steep banks. The next hairpin, ramping left, is when the real fun starts; it's achingly steep, and from here, for close to 300m the slope doesn't drop much below 15%. While you grind your way up, do make sure to look over your left shoulder to catch sight of The White Cliffs as you rise from the coast to finish at the brow next to the island with a boat on it.

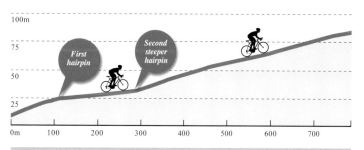

FACTFILE

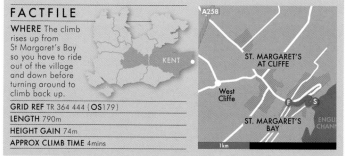

WHERE The climb rises up from St Margaret's Bay so you have to ride out of the village and down before turning around to climb back up.

GRID REF TR 364 444 (**OS**179)

LENGTH 790m

HEIGHT GAIN 74m

APPROX CLIMB TIME 4mins

EAST AND WEST SUSSEX

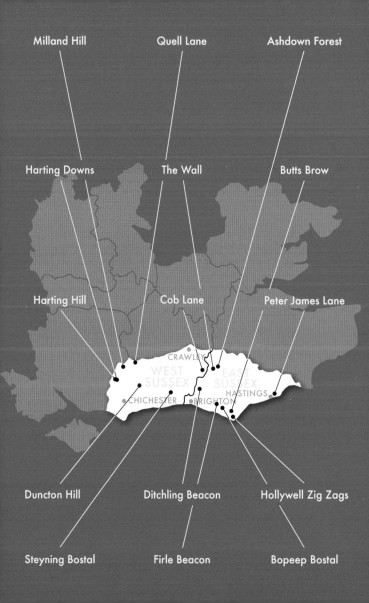

Milland Hill

Quell Lane

Ashdown Forest

Harting Downs

The Wall

Butts Brow

Harting Hill

Cob Lane

Peter James Lane

CRAWLEY

WEST SUSSEX

EAST SUSSEX

HASTINGS

CHICHESTER

BRIGHTON

Duncton Hill

Ditchling Beacon

Hollywell Zig Zags

Steyning Bostal

Firle Beacon

Bopeep Bostal

PETER JAMES LANE

FAIRLIGHT, EAST SUSSEX

Hastings is full of hills such as the very tough Old London Road, but this climb beats them all, and it's not packed with traffic. Swooping down from Pett Road you will carry plenty of momentum on to the lower slopes as you speed past the starting point: a small stone bridge in the hollow of the valley. Reasonably steep at first, round to the right then tougher still as it bends left. Then it backs off, and at that moment it leaves you thinking, was that it? The top doesn't seem that far away and you've hardly broken sweat, but rest assured, that's not it. Riding past the big houses, with big trees in their big gardens, the road begins to kink further round to the left, until it reveals the final long ramp of tarmac that just climbs steeper and steeper and steeper. The ramp stretches dead straight until almost the very end where it reaches close to 20% at the junction with Battery Hill, which is also well worth riding if you turn left.

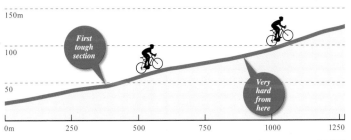

150m

First
tough
section

100

50

Very
hard
from
here

0m   250   500   750   1000   1250

FACTFILE

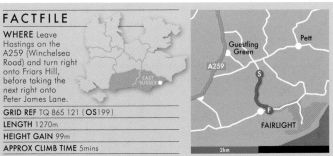

WHERE Leave Hastings on the A259 (Winchelsea Road) and turn right onto Friars Hill, before taking the next right onto Peter James Lane.

GRID REF TQ 865 121 (**OS**199)

LENGTH 1270m

HEIGHT GAIN 99m

APPROX CLIMB TIME 5mins

ASHDOWN FOREST

GROOMBRIDGE, EAST SUSSEX

If you leave Groombridge in a large group of riders, heading to the top of the Ashdown Forest, it fast becomes survival of the fittest as each ridge takes its toll. The climb's strength is the sum of its parts, it's a war of attrition that requires concentration and willpower to conquer. Exit Groombridge then turn south on to the B2188, dip down under a railway bridge and start the climb in the hollow. Your first rise is a stinging ramp before a short, fast descent to the base of the next ridge. Climb up to a junction on the left and continue on to pass through Friars Gate, on and on under the trees, getting steeper in places forcing you to grit your teeth a little. The first sign that you're getting close to the top is the large clearing where the sky opens up, cross this exposed stretch then plunge back under tree cover where the slope really kicks up. You then level for a brief rest before the last steep bit on your approach to the summit.

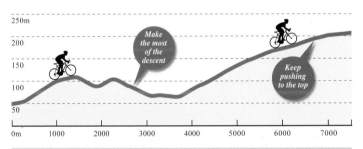

Make the most of the descent

Keep pushing to the top

FACTFILE

WHERE Head south from Groombridge on the B2110 then take the B2188 to Crowborough. Pass under the railway bridge then head up from the hollow.

GRID REF TQ 477 310 (OS188)

LENGTH 8500m

HEIGHT GAIN 174m

APPROX CLIMB TIME 21mins

THE WALL

FOREST ROW, EAST SUSSEX

Kidd's Hill, east of Coleman's Hatch in East Sussex, has been dubbed The Wall because when you reach the last section that is exactly what it feels like you're faced with. Begin this climb out of Newbridge. Crossing a bridge after a ford, the road ascends steadily. Bending slightly left it soon straightens, and there you have it: The Wall. Dead straight, uniformly steep, the road rises through the trees, no bends, no dips, no mercy. Why deviate when the quickest route to the top is a straight line? In this case it is one that leads to the light at the end of the tunnel of tree cover. Pedal rev by pedal rev you'll drag yourself towards this light – ever brighter as the pain increases – knowing once you reach it your torment will be almost at an end. Into the open, the gradient eases as you enter the beautiful heath on top of the Ashdown Forest with around 100m left to finish, just shy of the T-junction with the B2026.

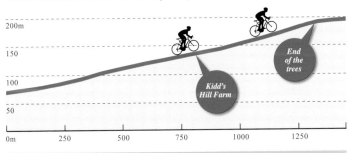

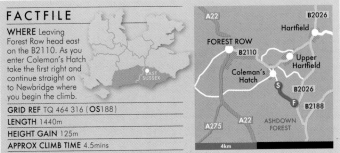

FACTFILE

WHERE Leaving Forest Row head east on the B2110. As you enter Coleman's Hatch take the first right and continue straight on to Newbridge where you begin the climb.

GRID REF TQ 464 316 (OS188)

LENGTH 1440m

HEIGHT GAIN 125m

APPROX CLIMB TIME 4.5mins

HOLYWELL ZIG ZAGS

EASTBOURNE, EAST SUSSEX

Twisting roads like this are few and far between in Britain so whenever I spot one on a map or read about one in a magazine my pulse quickens. If you lived in the mountains and were surrounded by such roads then you wouldn't bat an eyelid at these particular bends, but when you live in a land devoid of such treasures you have to seize the opportunity to ride them whenever it arises. The slopes of the Holywell Zig Zags lie on the B2103 and begin where the road leaves the seafront and heads inland. You turn first right, then left and this is where the climb is its steepest, rising to the brace of switchbacks. First left, then shortly after, right, set on a mildly testing slope you swing through the wonderful corners and up to the final bend. Now steep again, this corner arcs round a patch of open grassland before lining out for the push to the finish, which comes far too soon at the junction with Beachy Head Road.

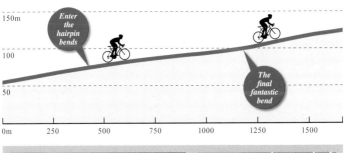

Enter the hairpin bends

The final fantastic bend

150m						
100						
50						
0m	250	500	750	1000	1250	1500

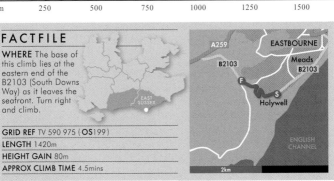

FACTFILE

WHERE The base of this climb lies at the eastern end of the B2103 (South Downs Way) as it leaves the seafront. Turn right and climb.

GRID REF	TV 590 975 (**OS**199)
LENGTH	1420m
HEIGHT GAIN	80m
APPROX CLIMB TIME	4.5mins

A259 EASTBOURNE
B2103 Meads B2103
F
S
Holywell
ENGLISH CHANNEL
2km

BUTTS LANE

WILLINGDON, EAST SUSSEX

As you approach this climb, riding through Willingdon, you catch flashes of the mound, peaking out between the houses; it doesn't look high enough to hurt you, but trust me, it is. It's a bit of a grind whichever way you approach Butts Lane so take it steady or you'll be in trouble later on. The start of the climb ramps up away from the junction and – ouch – it's steep and gets steeper all the way up and round the first left-hand 20% bend. After this you'll be able to sit down for a while but the gradient soon starts to increase again, getting harder and harder. It's back out of the saddle as you try to keep whatever gear you have turning on the unforgiving slope as it gradually bends right. Approaching the top, you're allowed a short rest as gravity momentarily relinquishes its grip before you bend left and head skyward up the wicked last 100m to the very welcome relief in the car park.

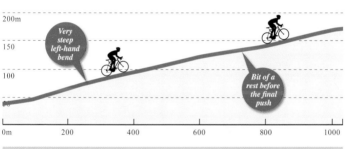

Very steep left-hand bend

Bit of a rest before the final push

FACTFILE

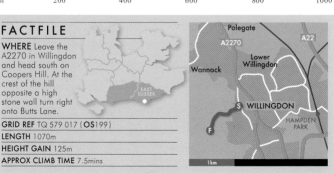

WHERE Leave the A2270 in Willingdon and head south on Coopers Hill. At the crest of the hill opposite a high stone wall turn right onto Butts Lane.

GRID REF TQ 579 017 (**OS**199)

LENGTH 1070m

HEIGHT GAIN 125m

APPROX CLIMB TIME 7.5mins

RATING

8/10

BOPEEP BOSTAL

SELMESTON, EAST SUSSEX

Having just ridden Firle Beacon, I thought that was as good as it could get for South-East England, but I have to say this beats it, just. Leave the A27 on Bopeep Lane and you sweep down to the base to start climbing from the hollow, the ridge ahead dominating the landscape. To warm your legs up, there's a short, sharp lip to tackle, and then the slope backs off for a while. Little by little, the gradient increases as the road bends 90 degrees left, then gently right up to a hard 20% bend that will push you well into the red. From here on it's a proper struggle as you grind up and up, away from the valley on the constant 14% gradient, which never eases, not for a moment. Through a couple of twists you'll catch sight of the final bend sweeping left. Cutting through the steep, grassy banks either side it will all but bring you to a halt as it delivers you into the full force of the wind coming off the English Channel. Stunning.

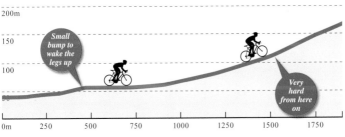

FACTFILE

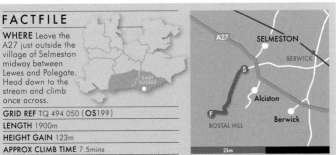

WHERE Leave the A27 just outside the village of Selmeston midway between Lewes and Polegate. Head down to the stream and climb once across.

GRID REF TQ 494 050 (**OS**199)

LENGTH 1900m

HEIGHT GAIN 123m

APPROX CLIMB TIME 7.5mins

FIRLE BOSTAL

WEST FIRLE, EAST SUSSEX

A stunning road, eerily quiet, set in fantastic scenery, and very hard to climb. Begin in the village of West Firle, where the main road sweeps to the left; leave it and head straight on, up Firle Bostal road. Ahead, the naked ridge lines the horizon, dotted with huge chalk bowls like bunkers on a giant golf course. The slope starts gently: there's a small rise, and then you plateau before the first serious climbing kicks in on a very uneven road making it impossible to settle into a rhythm. Ramping steeper up to a brow, the road kinks left and you reach the first of two significant rests. You're soon climbing again, in the shadow of the towering grassy banks and on a much better surface up to the next micro plateau. Time to catch your breath and prepare for the grind to the summit. Bending left it's consistently 10% to 12% from here on, but force upwards because your reward is one of the best views in Southern England.

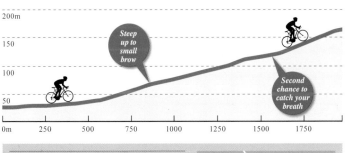

Steep up to small brow

Second chance to catch your breath

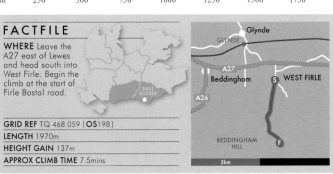

FACTFILE

WHERE Leave the A27 east of Lewes and head south into West Firle. Begin the climb at the start of Firle Bostal road.

GRID REF	TQ 468 059 (**OS**198)
LENGTH	1970m
HEIGHT GAIN	137m
APPROX CLIMB TIME	7.5mins

Glynde

GLYNDE

A27

Beddingham

WEST FIRLE

A26

BEDDINGHAM HILL

5km

DITCHLING BEACON

DITCHLING, EAST SUSSEX

Ditchling Beacon is the hill all inexperienced cyclists dread. As the sting in the tail of the London to Brighton charity ride, it holds the title of the climb that has forced more riders off their bikes than any other. It has also been included in many races, from the British National Hill Climb Championships to the Tour de France. Leaving Ditchling, the road begins to rise, priming your legs for the climb ahead. Crossing a junction, it banks left and ramps up steeply as you enter its snaking bends. Stepping up, steeper with each turn, you must ride with care as passing cars on this busy route will force you into the debris-filled gutters. Exiting the tree cover, the sky opens and the weald stretches in front of you, but this isn't the top. The pleasant view disappears as suddenly as it appeared where the road bends right into more tree cover, switching again before you emerge into the open, this time to play out the summit scenario for real.

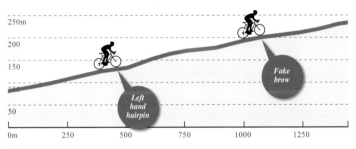

Left hand hairpin

Fake brow

FACTFILE

WHERE Pass through the village of Ditchling on the B2112. Cross the B2116 and take the first left onto the minor road, continue to the crossroads then climb.

GRID REF TQ 333 129 (**OS**198)

LENGTH 1445m

HEIGHT GAIN 132m

APPROX CLIMB TIME 6.5mins

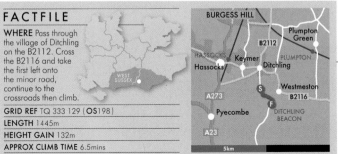

COB LANE

ARDINGLY, WEST SUSSEX

Before you climb Cob Lane you've got to tackle the treacherously steep, dirty, and narrow descent of the other side of Cob Lane – and then it's straight back up. What you face are 400m of pure, unadulterated, no-holds-barred suffering. To make things worse, when I last rode this wall I already had 100 miles in the legs and all I wanted to do was get off and walk, but I couldn't let it beat me. Cross the small stream at the base and almost right away it ramps up to 16% to where the climb leans right between the tall sloping banks. Rounding the bend, 16% approaches 20% for the toughest section up to the next curve in the road where it heads left. As you continue your struggle it does become slightly easier, but the road has one more card to play with a ferocious right-hand bend that leads you to the short approach to the blessed relief of the finish at the T-junction with the main road in Ardingly.

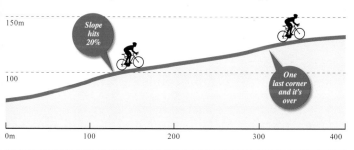

Slope hits 20%

One last corner and it's over

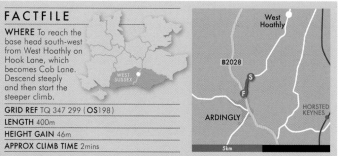

FACTFILE

WHERE To reach the base head south-west from West Hoathly on Hook Lane, which becomes Cob Lane. Descend steeply and then start the steeper climb.

GRID REF TQ 347 299 (OS198)

LENGTH 400m

HEIGHT GAIN 46m

APPROX CLIMB TIME 2mins

STEYNING BOSTAL

STEYNING, WEST SUSSEX

Running up and over the South Downs, Steyning Bostal is the final hurdle for many a ride heading to the coast. There are two ways to begin this climb, both starting from the centre of Steyning and both tough. The route raced each year in the Brighton Mitre CC Hill Climb uses Bostal Road, the southernmost of the two ascents, and, climbing reasonably steeply to begin with, you soon reach a 17% gradient sign. After crossing several raised ridges, the road twists left, then right, and is hard going through the bends. It next climbs through woodland then plateaus for a while, giving you just enough time for a brief recovery before you hit the second section. Angling hard to the left, the road – much smoother here – passes the junction for the alternate beginning before easing slightly. Passing an exposed chalkface on the right, it sweeps left, the gradient easing all the time before it turns right to finish opposite a small car park.

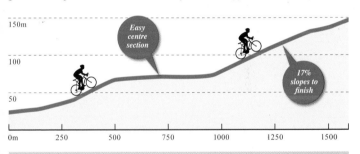

FACTFILE

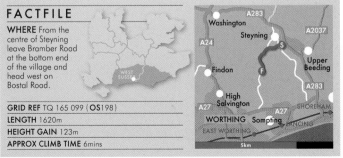

WHERE From the centre of Steyning leave Bramber Road at the bottom end of the village and head west on Bostal Road.

GRID REF TQ 165 099 (**OS**198)

LENGTH 1620m

HEIGHT GAIN 123m

APPROX CLIMB TIME 6mins

DUNCTON HILL

DUNCTON, WEST SUSSEX

Drop out from the centre of Duncton, over the bridge, and then start to climb sharply into the rest of the village; it's hard for a while, then you reach a brow and the road levels. For a while it crosses your mind that that might be it, but unless there's a tunnel through the ridge ahead you're in for a lot more hard work. A vast sweeping right-hand bend sits in front of you and, as you ride round it, becomes increasingly steeper until it straightens and settles into a solid 10% slope. In and out of the saddle I couldn't settle into a rhythm up here, as I found it consistently steeper than it looked! Three-quarters of the way up and there's a viewpoint on the right-hand side of the road where you can catch a glimpse of the valley, but you've more climbing ahead so stay focused. As the road begins to change course, round to the left, the summit will soon be in sight; head for the sign for Duncton Quarry, as the top lies just past it.

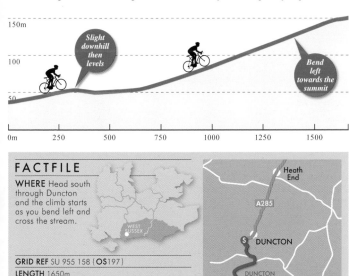

Slight downhill then levels

Bend left towards the summit

150m

100

50

0m   250   500   750   1000   1250   1500

FACTFILE

WHERE Head south through Duncton and the climb starts as you bend left and cross the stream.

WEST SUSSEX

Heath End

A285

S DUNCTON

DUNCTON DOWN

F

Sutton

2km

GRID REF SU 955 158 (OS197)	
LENGTH 1650m	
HEIGHT GAIN 114m	
APPROX CLIMB TIME 7.5mins	

QUELL LANE

FERNHURST, WEST SUSSEX

I found myself in this corner of Sussex to ride up Fernden Lane south out of Hasle-mere but happened to approach it from the south and ended up on Quell Lane. After weighing things up, and disregarding the superior length of Fernden Lane I decided Quell Lane was a more worthy inclusion. It's steeper, a purer climber's climb, and it's lined with some stunning properties – not that that should form part of the equation. Heading off at an angle from the main road the climb then bends left before sweeping round to the right and backing off slightly. Next is the first real tough stretch, round to the left then into a sharp, straight ramp up to a left-hand bend and an easing. The surface is now rough, overspread with gravel; in fact there are enough stones in the centre to cover a modest driveway. Keep to the clean tarmac, up the second really tough grind, then follow the road round to the left and finish as Fernden Lane begins.

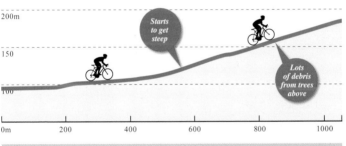

FACTFILE

WHERE Leave the A283 a junction south of the B2131 heading east and turn left at Gospel Green onto Jobsons Lane. Take your third right after that onto Quell Lane.

GRID REF SU 922 290 (OS186)	
LENGTH 1050m	
HEIGHT GAIN 88m	
APPROX CLIMB TIME 5mins	

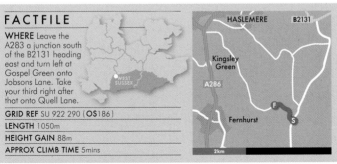

RATING
4/10

MILLAND HILL

MILLAND, WEST SUSSEX

I've tackled this hill a number of times in road races, and it provides an excellent finale for those riders who love to climb. Frustratingly, though, the finish line was always 100m past the summit, which allowed larger-built riders to get back on and charge past the skinny climbers with their fast-twitch fibres. The approach starts in the centre of Milland on the rough road that leads you to your fate, and, as the course begins to snake, the ridge comes into view, but the gradient is still mild. Bouncing along the patchwork of bodged repairs, you rise between tall banks topped with neat hedgerows. As the slope increases, the hedgerows are replaced by trees forming a V above and framing the finale: a 25% ramp up and under the small bridge. Rising increasingly steeper and hitting that 25% mark through the final left-hand bend, it requires a real effort to preserve a decent momentum up to the sudden and very welcome brow.

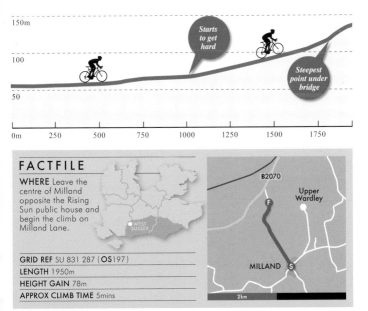

Starts to get hard

Steepest point under bridge

150m

100

50

0m   250   500   750   1000   1250   1500   1750

FACTFILE

WHERE Leave the centre of Milland opposite the Rising Sun public house and begin the climb on Milland Lane.

● WEST SUSSEX

GRID REF SU 831 287 (**OS**197)

LENGTH 1950m

HEIGHT GAIN 78m

APPROX CLIMB TIME 5mins

B2070

Upper Wardley

MILLAND S

2km

RATING
4/10

HARTING HILL

SOUTH HARTING, WEST SUSSEX

There are three routes rising out of South Harting up to the South Downs Way and I've included two in the book – this one and the one on page 106 – as I couldn't decide between them. This is the first and most direct way out of the village; starting at its centre you head south, past the church and up into the woods. Bending predominantly left, nothing spectacular happens for a while, but as you begin to bend right that's where things start to get tasty and the slope approaches 10%. Tough for a while, it backs off at the junction with the B2141 where the route splits – on the map resembling a giant serpent's tongue. Keep to the road you're on, and, as it bends right, you arrive at the super-steep ramp that maxes out at 13%. Saving the best till last, this 100m stretch is a struggle but it doesn't last long, and before you know it you reach the abrupt brow and can relax on level ground.

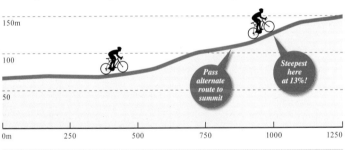

Pass alternate route to summit

Steepest here at 13%!

150m
100
50
0m   250   500   750   1000   1250

FACTFILE

WHERE Simply leave the centre of South Harting heading south on the B2146 and climb.

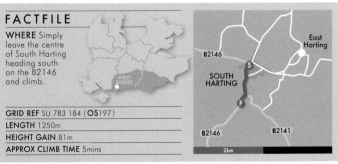

WEST SUSSEX

East Harting

B2146

SOUTH HARTING

B2146   B2141

2km

GRID REF SU 783 184 (**OS**197)

LENGTH 1250m

HEIGHT GAIN 81m

APPROX CLIMB TIME 5mins

RATING
5/10

HARTING DOWNS

SOUTH HARTING, WEST SUSSEX

Here is the second climb out of South Harting: the back route. Not quite as steep as the climb on the main road (p104), but with an extra 31m elevation, and, at 150m longer, it's just as hard if not harder. Also, being the quiet route, you'll have little or no traffic to contend with on your ascent, but alas a lot more debris and mud on this tiny road. There's a small zigzag away from the main road, and then you line up for the steady approach to the serious climbing which starts as the road bends right, up under the trees. Now up to 10%, it's a consistent grind, bending gradually left as it climbs in the permanent shade. When the road begins to turn right, you know you're getting closer to the top but at first there's no visible sign of the summit. Keep your eyes peeled, though, and you'll see cars flash across the junction ahead – this marks your salvation, your freedom from the grip of a very hard climb.

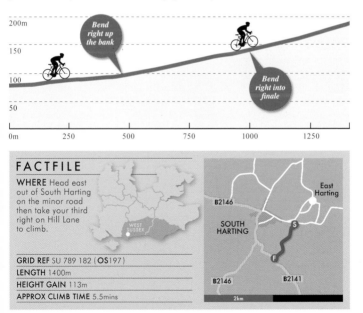

Bend right up the bank

Bend right into finale

FACTFILE

WHERE Head east out of South Harting on the minor road then take your third right on Hill Lane to climb.

GRID REF SU 789 182 (OS197)

LENGTH 1400m

HEIGHT GAIN 113m

APPROX CLIMB TIME 5.5mins

B2146
East Harting
SOUTH HARTING
S
B2146
B2141
F
2km

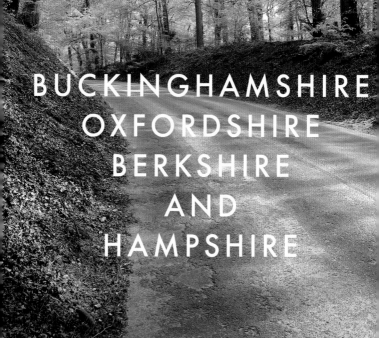

BUCKINGHAMSHIRE
OXFORDSHIRE
BERKSHIRE
AND
HAMPSHIRE

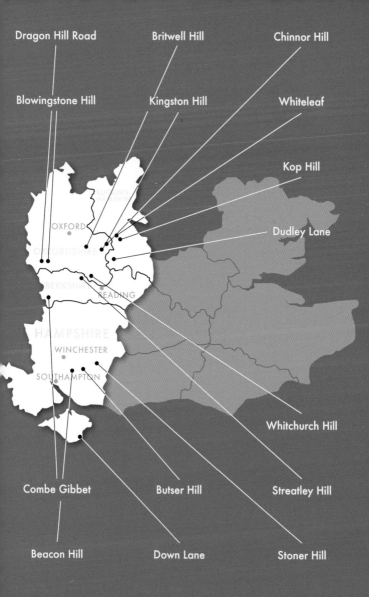

Dragon Hill Road

Britwell Hill

Chinnor Hill

Blowingstone Hill

Kingston Hill

Whiteleaf

Kop Hill

Dudley Lane

OXFORD

OXFORDSHIRE

BERKSHIRE

READING

HAMPSHIRE

WINCHESTER

SOUTHAMPTON

Whitchurch Hill

Combe Gibbet

Butser Hill

Streatley Hill

Beacon Hill

Down Lane

Stoner Hill

WHITELEAF

PRINCES RISBOROUGH, BUCKINGHAMSHIRE

This hill earned its fame as the key ingredient in a classic but sadly long gone British road race, the Archer Grand Prix. The inclusion of such a tough climb can make a race, and a race will gain a reputation because of it, attracting strong riders wanting to add their name to the list of winners. You start the ascent by turning off the A4010 from Monks Risborough, climbing from the off. Smooth and straight, the gradient increases gradually up to a left-hand kink where it slackens. The road twists a little, passing houses as it makes its way towards where the serious business begins. Banking right, the climb soon hits its 1-in-7 rating and the surface gets rougher as the road passes through tree cover. It continues steeply until the final left-hand bend alongside a small shelf of chalk, where you face one final kick before the gradient subsides and you reach the peak at the junction of the summit of Kop Hill.

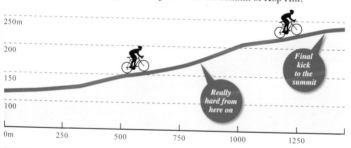

Really hard from here on

Final kick to the summit

FACTFILE

WHERE Travelling north-east from Princes Risborough on the A4010 reach Monks Risborough. Then take the first right before a school heading towards Whiteleaf.

GRID REF SP 814 043 (OS165)

LENGTH 1420m

HEIGHT GAIN 127m

APPROX CLIMB TIME 6mins

KOP HILL

You know you're in trouble when you get to the bottom of a hill and there's a neat white line painted across it, as this usually indicates the start line for a hill-climb event, and therefore what lies ahead will be a killer. There's a bit of a rise whichever way you approach the turn on to Kop Hill but you are allowed 100m of recovery before the real hard work begins. Up ahead, the slope hits you in three brutal sections, the first of which is the longest and will have you on the ropes by the time the respite arrives. Then, BAM! The second ramp hits you and you're on the canvas, your legs burning as they are pushed to maximum once more. Then, it eases again, but for a shorter stretch, then right away, BAM! This third increase in effort will deliver the knockout blow; now you have to beat the count to reach the safety of the top, which arrives in line with a 10% gradient sign – 10%! Someone is having a laugh: you can double that!

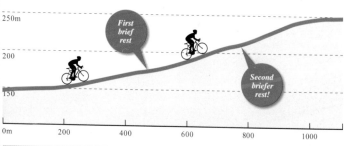

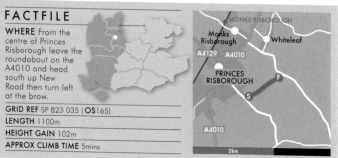

FACTFILE

WHERE From the centre of Princes Risborough leave the roundabout on the A4010 and head south up New Road then turn left at the brow.

GRID REF SP 823 035 (OS165)

LENGTH 1100m

HEIGHT GAIN 102m

APPROX CLIMB TIME 5mins

DUDLEY LANE

HAMBLEDEN, BUCKINGHAMSHIRE

Hidden in the twisting Buckinghamshire lanes and rising beneath the cries of the ever-present red kites, Dudley Lane is a fantastic test for the legs. As you reach the base, the sight of the climb snaking away up the hillside and vanishing into the woods at the top confronts you. Laid out in all its glory it is an imposing prospect, framed on the left by a line of trees and to the right by rolling grassland. The narrow, debris-covered road has a gentle beginning, and then as it gradually turns right the gradient increases. Meandering upwards, twisting gently left and right, the climb settles into a solid 7% slope until it disappears into the trees. Here you can relax, for a moment, before it ramps up once more on the approach to the winery. Through the small collection of buildings and away from temptation, the summit is still a good 800m further but it's a very gentle rise, so stick it in the big ring and wind it up!

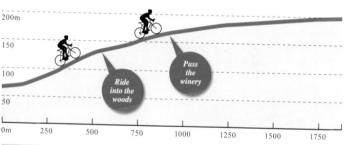

Ride into the woods

Pass the winery

200m
150
100
50
0m

250   500   750   1000   1250   1500   1750

FACTFILE

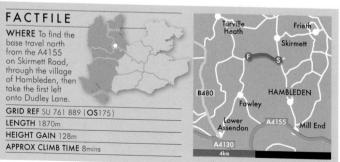

WHERE To find the base travel north from the A4155 on Skirmett Road, through the village of Hambleden, then take the first left onto Dudley Lane.

GRID REF SU 761 889 (**OS**175)

LENGTH 1870m

HEIGHT GAIN 128m

APPROX CLIMB TIME 8mins

RATING
4/10

CHINNOR HILL

CHINNOR, OXFORDSHIRE

This Chiltern Classic rises from the centre of Chinnor at the roundabout where Station Road leaves Oakley Road heading south. Rising up through the village, Station Road soon becomes Hill Road as you crest the small railway bridge then roll down to a roundabout that hinders your progress. Head straight across and you're on the climb proper; signposted Bledlow Ridge the road arcs slightly right before straightening as it settles into its long approach to the steep stuff. The gradient begins to get serious at the first of three right-hand kinks, each one ushering in tougher climbing up to a maximum of 8%. Following this hard work is what on paper looks like a hairpin bend, but is in fact a junction. Leave the road you're on and take the hard left. Wickedly steep at its apex, it delivers you to the final couple of hundred metres of climbing before the slope fades to nothing and you've reached the top.

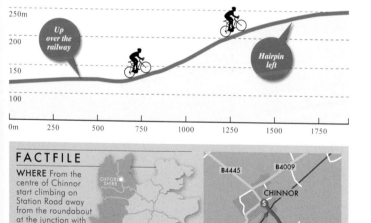

FACTFILE

WHERE From the centre of Chinnor start climbing on Station Road away from the roundabout at the junction with Oakley Road.

GRID REF SU 764 996 (OS165)

LENGTH 2050m

HEIGHT GAIN 129m

APPROX CLIMB TIME 7mins

KINGSTON HILL

KINGSTON BLOUNT, OXFORDSHIRE

There are many roads that criss-cross the Chiltern ridge; in fact you could cycle all day, up and down, and not ride the same climb twice. True, none of them are real killers; there are no 33% gradients, but a great climb doesn't always have to be steep. Start at the sign for the Kingston Blount Point-to-Point races, just before the gradient bites, and then really attack it. It's a short climb, so try to ride it at maximum from start to finish: keep the legs spinning, keep on top of your gear, and keep your effort high to power all the way through. The slope is gentle at first, but as the shadows of branches overhead replace the daylight, things get gradually tougher. Meandering left then right then left, the higher slopes are worn and pitted making your task harder, but maintain your momentum to finish just shy of the right-turn sign next to a private footpath on the left.

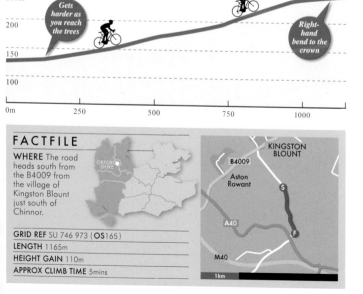

250m

Gets harder as you reach the trees

200

150

Right-hand bend to the crown

100

0m   250   500   750   1000

FACTFILE

WHERE The road heads south from the B4009 from the village of Kingston Blount just south of Chinnor.

GRID REF SU 746 973 (**OS**165)

LENGTH 1165m

HEIGHT GAIN 110m

APPROX CLIMB TIME 5mins

KINGSTON BLOUNT

B4009

Aston Rowant

A40

M40

1km

BRITWELL HILL

BRITWELL SALOME, OXFORDSHIRE

Heading south out of Britwell Salome, and upon first glance, this climb will force a double take; from a distance this arrow-straight line of tarmac bisecting the empty hillside looks like a wall. The closer you get, however, the less daunting its apparent sheer face becomes, and once you've rolled down to its base it looks far more manageable, which will be a huge relief. Although the direction is uniform, the gradient is a little more varied with the first 100 or so meters easy, then with each subsequent 100m it ramps up that little bit more to its 12.5% maximum. Each time the gradient increases you'll click up a sprocket to keep the legs turning and will breathe a little harder to satisfy the demand for oxygen. Hopefully you'll have enough teeth on the cassette, and strong enough lungs, to get you to the brow, which arrives abruptly, sitting entrenched between the high banks either side.

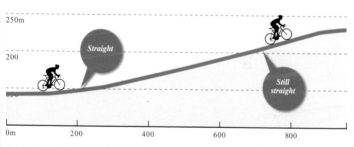

Straight

Still straight

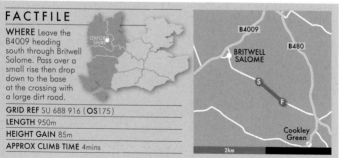

FACTFILE

WHERE Leave the B4009 heading south through Britwell Salome. Pass over a small rise then drop down to the base at the crossing with a large dirt road.

GRID REF SU 688 916 (OS175)

LENGTH 950m

HEIGHT GAIN 85m

APPROX CLIMB TIME 4mins

RATING 4/10

WHITCHURCH HILL

WHITCHURCH, OXFORDSHIRE

Approaching this hill from the top, not that you would if you intended to ride up it, but if you did, you'd be met by a mighty, unsightly sign warning you of its 20% gradients and twisting bends. In truth this road has neither. Yes there are curves and yes it's pretty steep at one point, but there is nothing to warrant the hysterics of this sign. Heading to the base from Pangbourne, you first have to cross the quaint little toll bridge – relax, it's free for bikes – then once in Whitchurch the climb begins to rise past the Greyhound Inn. It's not long before you hit the tough bit as the road narrows, squeezing to a single carriageway, and here it's close to 20% but not quite. Once through, you reach the bulk of the climb set on a 10% to 12% slope; grind on and up then the road sweeps right, then left, at which point you will catch sight of the summit, and that alarmist sign, just before the turning to the village of Whitchurch Hill.

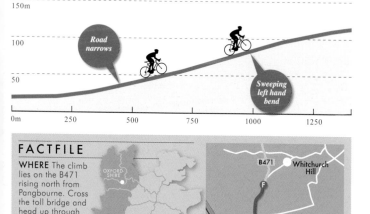

150m

100

50

0m   250   500   750   1000   1250

Road narrows

Sweeping left hand bend

FACTFILE

WHERE The climb lies on the B471 rising north from Pangbourne. Cross the toll bridge and head up through Whitchurch-on-Thames.

GRID REF SU 636 784 (OS175)

LENGTH 1400m

HEIGHT GAIN 90m

APPROX CLIMB TIME 5mins

B471   Whitchurch Hill

F

WHITCHURCH -ON-THAMES

S

PANGBOURNE

Pangbourne   A329   Purley on Thames

A340

2km

BLOWINGSTONE HILL

KINGSTON LISLE, OXFORDSHIRE

The first time I rode this hill, and unaware it lay ahead, I'd minutes beforehand consumed a giant jacket potato filled with beans and cheese at a café stop in Wantage. Now you don't need to be a sports scientist to work out that this isn't the best prep for an eyeballs-out race with your clubmates up a 10% ramp – thankfully I managed to keep it down! As you turn off the B4507 you begin the climb almost right away, and almost right away it's hard – all but dead straight up the wide, bumpy road. The gradient is pretty much a constant, just shifting incrementally up or down from the 10% median to either fractionally increase or decrease the pain as the views to your right grow in grandeur. Nearing the top and you've the killer finish to face. The final 50m are the hardest of all up to the awful false flat, which you must push through to the sign on the right that marks the end.

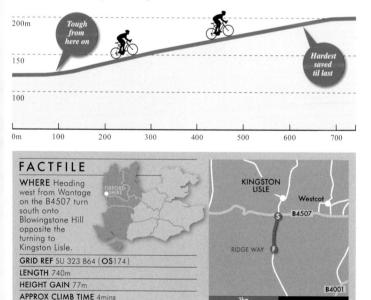

200m   **Tough from here on**

150

Hardest saved til last

100

0m   100   200   300   400   500   600   700

FACTFILE

WHERE Heading west from Wantage on the B4507 turn south onto Blowingstone Hill opposite the turning to Kingston Lisle.

GRID REF SU 323 864 (OS174)

LENGTH 740m

HEIGHT GAIN 77m

APPROX CLIMB TIME 4mins

KINGSTON LISLE

Westcot

B4507

S

RIDGE WAY   F

B4001

2km

RATING
5/10

DRAGON HILL ROAD

WOOLSTONE, OXFORDSHIRE

Dragon Hill Road has no earthly place here – climbing out of the Vale of the White Horse, it is as if it's been transported rock by rock from the Peak District. This little patch of isolated beauty with its narrow chalk-stained road is a real find, and to boot, seriously tough to climb. Essentially, it is a road to nowhere, a detour; you leave the B4507, ride the climb then loop back past the White Horse visitors car park to rejoin the same road. The climb starts as you leave the main road. Cross a rickety cattle grid and make your way up the tight road as it enters the beautiful, almost vertical, grassy banks. The gradient is at worst 1-in-6 and eases about halfway before reaching its steepest stretch after a 90-degree right-hand bend. There's little sign of the White Horse – it is way above you – so keep one eye on the road and the other on the awesome view as you roll to a finish at a National Trust car park.

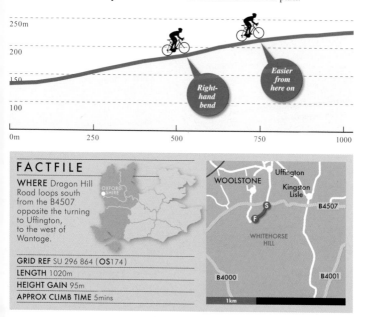

FACTFILE

WHERE Dragon Hill Road loops south from the B4507 opposite the turning to Uffington, to the west of Wantage.

GRID REF SU 296 864 (**OS**174)

LENGTH 1020m

HEIGHT GAIN 95m

APPROX CLIMB TIME 5mins

RATING
5/10

STREATLEY HILL

STREATLEY, BERKSHIRE

Streatley Hill is an infamous climb in this region, and its inclusion in the 2008 professional Tour of Britain only strengthened its status as a classic. Rising from the idyllic villages of Streatley and Goring, this unforgiving stretch of road begins to climb as soon as you leave the A417, which bisects them. It is steep to the first bend, a slight left, then steeper still for a short section that takes you to the next slight left-hander, where the gradient increases subtly once more. Apart from numerous sunken iron drainage grilles close to the gutter, the surface is good, almost smooth in places. Passing a driveway on the left, you reach the final push and the hardest section. As the road bends right you can picture the summit but have to work very hard to reach it as the road banks left, topping out just past a National Trust car park. Take care here, as this is a busy spot with cars turning to enter and exit the car park.

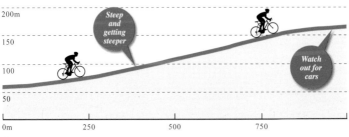

FACTFILE

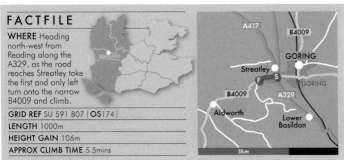

WHERE Heading north-west from Reading along the A329, as the road reaches Streatley take the first and only left turn onto the narrow B4009 and climb.

GRID REF SU 591 807 (**OS**174)

LENGTH 1000m

HEIGHT GAIN 106m

APPROX CLIMB TIME 5.5mins

COMBE GIBBET

HUNGERFORD, BERKSHIRE

With stunning views from the top, Combe Gibbet, or Inkpen Hill, is a real treat to climb. Heading south from the village of Inkpen and into a valley, the climb starts adjacent to an abandoned farm building. Gentle at first, the road continues straight and smooth, but cast your eyes upwards and atop the hill you can see the gibbet. Erected to execute criminals, or more often to display their bodies, it dates from 1676 and adds a sinister context to this beautiful ascent. The gentle rise bends left and climbs fiercely beneath a canopy of trees, where the surface starts to deteriorate. Once out the other side of the tree cover, the climb feels easier but it's the surface that has improved, not the gradient that's slackened. The road does ease slightly. But no sooner has it done so than it kicks up again for the hard pull to the top, where you are treated to a fantastic panorama of the Thames Valley, and, in an instant, you forget the effort.

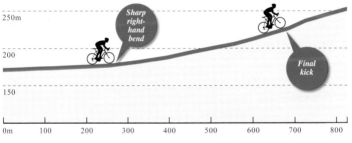

Sharp right-hand bend

Final kick

250m

200

150

0m   100   200   300   400   500   600   700   800

FACTFILE

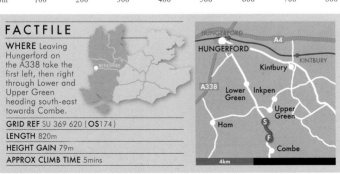

WHERE Leaving Hungerford on the A338 take the first left, then right through Lower and Upper Green heading south-east towards Combe.

GRID REF SU 369 620 (OS174)

LENGTH 820m

HEIGHT GAIN 79m

APPROX CLIMB TIME 5mins

RATING 2/10

STONER HILL

STEEP, HAMPSHIRE

This is one of those rare British climbs, which, even though it's just for a short while, gives you a glimpse of what it feels like to climb a mountain. That might sound a bit far-fetched but with its comfortable gradient and wonderful scenery, use a bit of imagination and you could be in the Alps, for 2 kilometres. Starting in the village of Steep – even though it never is – the road climbs gently at first then begins to rise up on what, when I visited, was the most wonderful new surface. If you'd studied the road on paper before you set off, you would have seen the two sharp bends towards the top suggesting this to be where the action arrived. Depending on your persuasion, however, you will either be relieved or disappointed as the first left-hander marks the end of the best of the climbing. In fact it's pan-flat between them but does pick up for the finale to end this stunning climb where a road joins from the right.

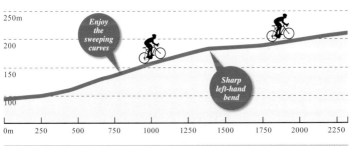

Enjoy the sweeping curves

Sharp left-hand bend

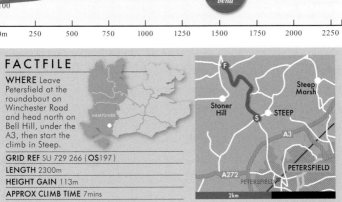

FACTFILE

WHERE Leave Petersfield at the roundabout on Winchester Road and head north on Bell Hill, under the A3, then start the climb in Steep.

GRID REF SU 729 266 (**OS**197)

LENGTH 2300m

HEIGHT GAIN 113m

APPROX CLIMB TIME 7mins

RATING
7/10

BUTSER HILL

EAST MEON, HAMPSHIRE

WOW, this is a beast. But the views from the top must be among the best in the South-East – it's just that you have one hell of a climb to reach them! Start as Harvesting Lane leaves Oxenbourne Lane and the first kilometre is pretty flat; in fact, you could argue you're not actually climbing but trust me, you are. Soon, over to your left you will see the huge radio mast on top of the hill and ahead you'll catch sight of the road rearing skywards through some trees. From here on it's hard, and when you reach the vicious right-hand bend the suffering really starts. Horribly steep, but with awesome views all around you crawl up and up its 11% slope for an age. Nearing the summit you'll see a small ridge on the road surface. After this the gradient drops, only by 1%, but this is enough to ease the pain, and you can start to relax on the approach to the top and the junction with the South Downs Way.

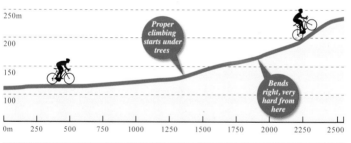

Proper climbing starts under trees

Bends right, very hard from here

250m
200
150
100

0m   250   500   750   1000   1250   1500   1750   2000   2250   2500

FACTFILE

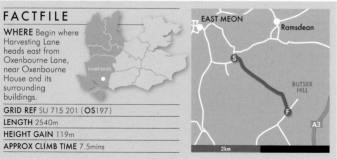

WHERE Begin where Harvesting Lane heads east from Oxenbourne Lane, near Oxenbourne House and its surrounding buildings.

GRID REF SU 715 201 (**OS**197)

LENGTH 2540m

HEIGHT GAIN 119m

APPROX CLIMB TIME 7.5mins

EAST MEON
Ramsdean
BUTSER HILL
A3
2km

BEACON HILL

EXTON, HAMPSHIRE

Be warned, I managed to take two wrong turns at the base of this climb as I navigated though Exton, so pay attention. Leave the A32 and head into the village; first take a left on to Beacon Hill Lane, then as that road veers left carry straight on up an incredibly narrow lane to the junction with The White Way. Turning right here, you are now on track: very gentle to start with, and then, as the road changes course up the ridge, the gradient increases to its almost constant 7%. Not punishing but not a breeze, it creeps up the hillside, gradually lifting you from the valley and revealing the wonderful views over the Downs. Further up, the road starts to bend gradually left around an ever-lasting corner that keeps any indication of what lies ahead a mystery. When it does straighten up, you pass the beacon for which the hill is named, but you've still a short way to go to finish just before the junction with Beacon Hill Lane.

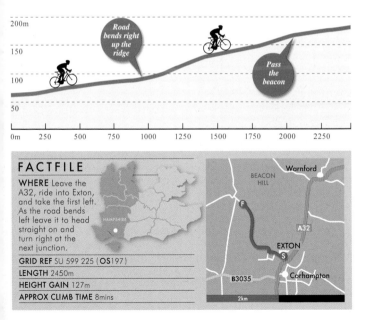

FACTFILE

WHERE Leave the A32, ride into Exton, and take the first left. As the road bends left leave it to head straight on and turn right at the next junction.

GRID REF SU 599 225 (**OS**197)

LENGTH 2450m

HEIGHT GAIN 127m

APPROX CLIMB TIME 8mins

DOWN LANE

VENTNOR, ISLE OF WIGHT

The small town of Ventnor on the Isle of Wight is packed with vicious little hills and zigzagging streets, and, quite literally, to top them all off is Down Lane. It's a silky smooth, twisting, narrow road that's almost 20% for its first half and steeper still in the corners as it heads to the high ground from where you are rewarded with excellent views over the English Channel. Although a serious climb in itself, for a greater challenge you can ride all the way from the beach to the summit by combining these three excellent roads. Starting from the western end of the Esplanade, take the very short but perfectly formed 25% Bath Road, make a left at the top then right at the T-junction on to the A3055. The next left brings you on to the quite unique hairpins of Zig Zag Road that lead you to the junction with Ocean View Road. Turn right then follow round the corner taking your first right to start the final climb – Down Lane.

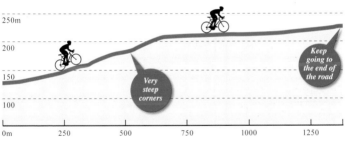

Very steep corners

Keep going to the end of the road

FACTFILE

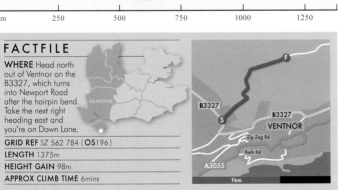

WHERE Head north out of Ventnor on the B3327, which turns into Newport Road after the hairpin bend. Take the next right heading east and you're on Down Lane.

GRID REF SZ 562 784 (OS196)

LENGTH 1375m

HEIGHT GAIN 98m

APPROX CLIMB TIME 6mins

RIDE THEM ALL

YES, ALL OF THEM!

As always the book finishes with the checklist, and if you already own the original *100 Greatest Cycling Climbs* and its sequel, *Another 100 Greatest Cycling Climbs*, then you may be able to tick a few off right away. If not, don't feel overwhelmed, there are only sixty hills here to conquer and they will always be there, barring any major tectonic activity. And, as many are in close proximity to each other, you should be able to bag a handful from one area in a single day. So have fun planning your routes and adventures, stay safe, and remember to avoid Box Hill on a Sunday morning!

LONDON AND ESSEX

Hill	Date Ridden	Time
North Hill		
Old Church Hill		
Mott Street		
Swain's Lane		
Muswell Hill		
College Road		

SURREY AND KENT

Hill	Date Ridden	Time
Barhatch Lane		
Combe Lane		
White Downs		
Leith Hill		
Coldharbour Lane		
Box Hill		

Hill	Date Ridden	Time
Hilltop Lane		
Chalkpit Lane		
White Lane		
Brasted Hill		
Star Hill		
Toy's Hill		
York's Hill		
Row Dow		
Exedown Road		
Vigo Hill		
Birling Hill		
Vanity Lane		
Boxley Hill		
Castle Hill		
Hollingbourne Hill		
White Hill		
Lympne Hill		
Bay Hill		

EAST AND WEST SUSSEX

Hill	Date Ridden	Time
Peter James Lane		
Ashdown Forest		
The Wall		
Holywell Zig Zags		
Butts Lane		
Bopeep Bostal		

Hill	Date Ridden	Time
Firle Bostal		
Ditchling Beacon		
Cob Lane		
Steyning Bostal		
Duncton Hill		
Quell Lane		
Milland Hill		
Harting Hill		
Harting Downs		

BUCKINGHAMSHIRE, OXFORDSHIRE, BERKSHIRE AND HAMPSHIRE

Hill	Date Ridden	Time
Whiteleaf		
Kop Hill		
Dudley Lane		
Chinnor Hill		
Kingston Hill		
Britwell Hill		
Whitchurch Hill		
Blowingstone Hill		
Dragon Hill Road		
Streatley Hill		
Combe Gibbet		
Stoner Hill		
Butser Hill		
Beacon Hill		
Down Lane		

Ride them all.

WWW.100CLIMBS.CO.UK

British climbing guides already available

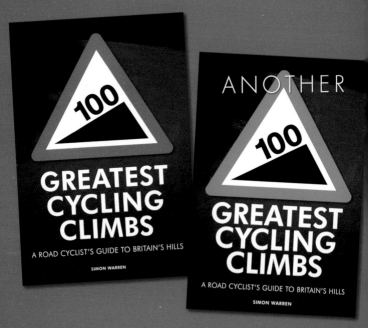

100 Greatest Cycling Climbs and
Another 100 Greatest Cycling Climbs

F

FRANCES LINCOLN LIMITED
PUBLISHERS